Tocqueville's America

Tocqueville's America
The Great Quotations

edited by

Frederick Kershner, Jr.

with an introduction and annotations

Ohio University Press
Athens, Ohio
London

Introduction, annotations, format
Copyright © 1983 by Cooper Industries

Library of Congress Catalog Card Number 83-60265

ISBN 0-8214-0750-3

Printed in the United States of America

Tocqueville's America was
commissioned and funded by Cooper
Industries in observance of its one
hundred and fiftieth anniversary.

Table of Contents

Acknowledgement

Most of the quotations in this book are from *Democracy in America*, by Alexis de Tocqueville, translated by Henry Reeve, revised by Francis Bowen, and edited by Phillips Bradley, copyrighted in 1945 and renewed in 1973 by Alfred A. Knopf. Reprinted by permission of the publisher.

Other quotations were taken from Tocqueville, *Journey to America*, translated by George Lawrence and edited by J. P. Mayer for the Yale University Press in 1959, and from Tocqueville, *European Revolution* and *Correspondence with Gobineau,* edited and translated by John Lukacs for Doubleday Anchor Books, Doubleday and Co., New York in 1959, reprinted by permission.

Introduction:
A Young Man and His Book

Behind every book there must be at least one author, a human being of flesh and blood, colorful traits, and revealing experiences. Such was indeed true of *Democracy in America*. The young Frenchman who planned this famous work and carried it through to completion was named Alexis Charles Henri Maurice Clerel, the Comte de Tocqueville. His life was comparatively short, from 1805 to 1859, being terminated abruptly by a sudden wasting disease, probably tuberculosis.[1]

The high points of Tocqueville's career were a brief magistracy in Paris (1827–32), the trip to America (1831–32) which resulted in his book, followed by a political period (1839–52) with several terms in the French Chamber of Deputies and a brief stint as Minister of Foreign Affairs under the Second Republic. Otherwise, he was a country gentleman of independent means who traveled frequently, wrote history now and then, and corresponded with many famous friends. Beyond a doubt, the American trip and book constitute the crowning events of his career.

One of the most surprising sides of Tocqueville, as author of *Democracy in America*, was his youth. Contemporaries were immediately struck by it. One termed his book "the work of a very young man";[2] another commented upon his "boyishness," with a warning that, despite having produced "one of the wisest works of modern thought, he was still a philosopher of seven and twenty. . . ."[3] Tocqueville himself wrote from America to his family that he and his close friend Beaumont "laughed in their sleeves . . . to think what insignificant men they were at home and what great men they were abroad. . . ."[4] Nonetheless, on public occasions they invariably behaved with dignity and courtesy.

Youth, itself, is no disgrace, of course. Many leaders of action in the American Revolution were younger than Tocqueville when they first came into the public eye—Jefferson, Hamilton, Madison, and Monroe, for example. But one hardly expects to find such tender years in the creator of so sophisticated an analysis as *Democracy in America*. Nevertheless, a respected authority believes that Tocqueville's creative product "was nothing but the execution of thoughts and projects conceived in his youth," even before he visited America.[5] What a dazzling example for bright, ambitious college students—or others young in heart and mind—today!

Compounded with insufficient age was insufficient education, even by the standards of Tocqueville's own lifetime. Of two American critics writing tributes to Tocqueville upon his death, one says "his education does not appear to have been well cared for," and the other terms it "irregular."[6] Yet, for the aristocracy, this sort of education had been traditional enough for many centuries, namely, home tutoring plus a few years of clerically or state-sponsored professional training. In fact, Tocqueville *was* well-educated, by means of family training, by reading in his own library, by travel abroad, and by a large correspondence with leaders of thought and opinion in the Western world.[7] One thinks especially of Franklin, and to a large extent Edison, Lincoln, and Henry Clay, as ready examples of this same autodidactic or self-education process. Perhaps self-education is better suited for developing great leadership than is completion of a college degree, if continuing to learn and develop after the end of formal instruction be the measure of success.

President Daniel Coit Gilman of Johns Hopkins University summed it up best almost a century ago:

> He cannot be accounted for. . . . Without unusual training, without the advantages of university education, without the preparation which a great library might afford, without the stimulus of poverty, the spur of ambition or the obligations of office, and even without instructions as to the methods of inquiry which he should initiate and follow, Tocqueville, at an age when most young men are about to begin, under the protection of their seniors, a professional life, conceived and matured by himself a plan for studying upon a vast area, in a foreign land the language of which was unfamiliar to him, the processes and results of democratic government, that he might bring home to his native land the lessons of political prosperity. The success which attended this youthful endeavor . . . is proof that he was a man of rare gifts. . . ."[8]

Also, he was flagrantly aristocratic. The family could trace back its Norman origins—in the St. Lo area—almost a thousand years; a Clerel had fought with William the Conqueror at Hastings. More recently, his most prominent grandparents and relatives had been guillotined during the Terror. His parents escaped the same fate by hours, when Robespierre was unexpectedly overthrown, an experience which turned his twenty-one-year-old future father's hair snow white overnight.[9] So although the younger Tocqueville was clearly an aristocrat, this did him more good than harm with Americans, for he was an aristocrat who had suffered, "who recognized that the day of his order was done," and shed no tears over it.[10] In Reeve's words, "His own ideal of social excellence and political greatness lay precisely in the combination of aristocratic tastes with popular interests. . . ."[11] The future was his major concern, and he saw no place there for old-style aristocracy as a class.

While Tocqueville was an intellectual theorizer, he was a pragmatic, action-oriented one. Indeed, how could any student of future trends help but be theoretical to a large degree? Add to this that he was talented in conversation (and in listening), a man who made friends easily and kept them unusually well, an unobtrusive moralist and "objectively pro-American."[12] It is little wonder so many Americans approved of this slight, pale little Frenchman with his expressive black eyes.

And he liked them. Very briefly he even considered settling in the United States, we are told.[13] The moment quickly passed. Tocqueville was too much the French patriot to abandon his country for any other.

If Tocqueville the man was remarkable, his book was equally so. By 1835, over twelve hundred Frenchmen had already written about America; not one of them had achieved an impact remotely approaching that of *Democracy in America*.[14] Almost overnight the new book was a sensation—Volume 1, that is, with Volume 2 coming five years later.[15] Both were translated into many different European languages with minimum delay. A primary reason for the book's success was its massive use of keen, reflective generalizations. These judgments were based upon hard data, simply stated, terse, and (in Tocqueville's own words) interpreted not in "metaphysical" abstractions but rather "the plainest common sense."[16] As a result, *Democracy in America* has become from that day onward a mine of triple-distilled wisdom about American society and life. A modern critic, David Riesman, has commented: *"Democracy in America* is singularly free of detailed descriptions of peoples and places . . . a work not of observation but interpretation. . . . No other visitor has to my knowledge been so little distracted by the accidental and so sensitive to implication."[17]

This was no single-theme essay designed to propagandize or convert. Instead, it was a composite of small details and large interpretations, all set down reflectively and with great insight.[18] Nothing escaped Tocqueville's attention, one feels. And his objectivity was striking in that Jacksonian era of passionate party warfare, for Tocqueville's "view of America was constructive and non-partisan."[19] He was proud of his impartiality, on one occasion writing to Henry Reeve about his reviewers, "They insist on making me a party man, and I am not. They give me passions, when I have only opinions, or rather the only passions I have are love of liberty and human dignity. . . . They endow me alternately with aristocratic and democratic prejudices."[20]

It was true enough, and Americans felt this. In 1841 a book of similar size appeared, written by a French engineer long resident in America, issued in Paris by Tocqueville's own publisher, Gosselin. In spite of being strongly partial to American democracy, this new book was not well received. Said the American reviewer: "We are not sure that we like it the better on that account. For, after all, the great merit of M. de Tocqueville consists in the singular justness of his analysis, and the impartiality with which he weighs in even scales the good and the bad consequences of our form of Government."[21]

In still another respect *Democracy in America* seems modern to us, many years ahead of its time. That is, it analyzed American culture in an international comparative context. Comparative history, politics, and economics are all post-World War II developments, essentially, so one can hardly blame the nineteenth-century critics for failing to recognize a creative departure like this for what it was. Some of them accused Tocqueville of using America as a mere convenience for lecturing the French. Others were flattered to be included on equal terms with France in a discussion of the worldwide importance of powerful ideas like democracy and equality.[22] Today the comparative emphasis, now so popular, has played its part in the revival of *Democracy in America* as a source of insight into modern American life and problems.

Style and method also contribute to its persistent attraction for later generations. While Tocqueville's style in the book was detached and precise (unlike his informal, easy, and sometimes opinionated flow in the "Travel Notes," from which *Democracy in America* was largely derived), it possessed a full measure of Gallic literary grace and pungency. Henry Steele Commager concludes that one of its great merits was a style "felicitous and even brilliant. There are no purple patches, there are few epigrams, but there is throughout, a luminous clarity, a resiliency, a masculine toughness, that contrasts with the rhetoric [of all his major foreign critic competitors]."[23]

Method is hardly the most fascinating side of any subject. However, there are aspects of Tocqueville's method in the work which are typically original and stimulating. Let us consider his use of the interview technique. Tocqueville did not rely solely upon books and records for information. He went beyond the printed word to interview the more important actors or authors themselves. His conversations were designed to correct, clarify, and enrich impressions gained from study of the original sources, not to serve as a lazy man's substitute for true research. Distrustful of his memory, he kept meticulous written records of these interviews, much like tape-recorded sessions today. In fact (although this has attracted little or no professional attention), Tocqueville was practicing oral history to the limit permitted by insufficient technology, long before Allan Nevins created this modern method in 1945.

Another startlingly modern technique, although unheard of at the time he used it, was the "sociological approach." This meant that Tocqueville did not stop with political analysis, but gave almost equal attention to economic, social, and cultural aspects of American democracy. Today, the fashionable *Annales* school of French historians enjoys the credit for a "new" kind of history which is little different in principle from Tocqueville's effort to paint the balanced picture of a total society, employing what we now recognize as "models," "ideal types," and "systems theory" for his purposes.[24]

As one might guess, many academic disciplines now rush to claim him—history, political science, sociology, and social science—and there is justice in each plea.

Tocqueville wrote only three full books—*Democracy in America* (1835, 1840), the *Recollections* (1850) and *The Old Regime and the Revolution* (1856). Many of his letters and other works have been published, as well as the incomplete early chapters of a projected book, *The European Revolution,* which was interrupted by his death. Of these, *Democracy in America* is and always has been by far the most influential, the most often published, and the most widely read. In England, France, and many other European states it was accepted as a classic from the very first. Thereafter, as the prime authority on the American experiment, it ensured that the new nation would never again be taken lightly by Europeans. Americans read it, too, and as late as 1900 it was still being used by many schools and colleges for textbook purposes in various courses.[25]

However, the popularity of *Democracy in America,* while never vanishing, has experienced high and low tides. The first high tide of esteem lasted through Tocqueville's lifetime and a decade or so following. From 1835 to 1870, the book's world importance was everywhere recognized, and it was much praised by radicals and conservatives alike. Intense interest at this time was constantly refueled by English fears of the possible Americanization of British life, French fears of American radicalism, and American satisfaction over the unanticipated respectability conferred upon them. Significantly, it was Volume 1 with its greater specific detail, its flattering and optimistic coloration, its political and institutional focus—all suitable as an introduction to the American system—which enjoyed the greatest popularity. Volume 2 was thought inferior because too speculative, theoretical, and hard to prove by detailed factual evidence.[26]

"Then," says Robert Nisbet, "the book fell upon hard times." It lost favor with the young, and academicians turned from Tocqueville to Lord Bryce and his *American Commonwealth.*[27] Even so, Woodrow Wilson in a review of Bryce's great book, commented perceptively, "It will hardly be accounted a disparagement of Mr. Bryce's style to say it is inferior to de Tocqueville's; the thoughts it [Bryce's book] has to convey, the meanings it has to suggest, belong to quite another class than that to which de Tocqueville's judgments must be assigned. . . . Mr. Bryce does not feel called upon to compete with de Tocqueville in the field in which de Tocqueville is possibly beyond rivalry."[28]

These late Victorian and early twentieth-century years were marked by the coming into fashion of imperialism and naked power politics, poisonously in Europe and as a milder, seductive wine in the United States. The trend was accompanied by growing skepticism about the future of democracy as a viable political and social system. For famous old books to lose popularity under such circumstances is commonplace. That *Democracy in America* should retain a significant core of appreciative readers despite the receding tide of interest was unusual and indicative.

Then, during the 1930s, the ebbing of interest halted, and the postwar years have witnessed a renewal of his reputation. Most authorities believe that this revival, not just in academic circles, but among thoughtful people everywhere, is well short of cresting today. To be sure, we do not read Tocqueville in the same way we once did. The descriptive details, the cautious optimism, and the qualified endorsement of American democracy for emulation elsewhere, which are to be found in Volume 1, are still appreciated, of course. But it is Tocqueville's fascinating speculations about the meaning of democracy and its great *future* problems, contained in the once-deprecated and now praised Volume 2, that account for the new tide of American and world interest. Some have even suggested that Tocqueville may be the true key to moving beyond Marx in our plans for a better world.[29]

In retrospect, it would appear that the first revival of interest in Tocqueville, before and during World War II, was political in focus. Many bright young students, starting with doubts about *capitalistic* democracy, became even more fearful of *mass totalitarian* democracy as manifested in fascism, and in the paternalistic superstate of Soviet democracy where the rule of one class seemed a potential tyranny worse than the class warfare it sought to replace. For such reflections, the words of Tocqueville were illuminating and suggestive. Some few began for the first time to consider the New Deal as a transition period, rather than as an ultimate state utopia.[30]

But as the memory of World War II faded, the faith in political solutions declined also. New developments made American interest shift to social and cultural aspects of democracy, especially at home, but related to the world society from which we no longer felt so far removed. One such development was the achievement of widespread affluence, without the happiness we had expected from it. Instead, prosperity brought in its train something called "alienation," the erosion of business and professional ethics (Tocqueville called it "honor"), permanent inflation, cultural debasement (or kitsch), the devitalization of religion, and the "managing of consent."

Does mass democracy mean the death of quality, excellence, and merit throughout society? Does democratic equality dictate a mindless anthill scramble for an "equal cut of the gravy" without regard to contributory input? Do democracy and patriotism still possess dynamism and persuasive power sufficient for natural leaders to redirect our movement away from such unattractive yet all-too-possible outcomes within a democratic society? Or must we sacrifice democracy on the altar of survival? Tocqueville speaks to these issues in prophetic, thought-provoking ways.

Tocqueville's *Democracy in America* is not the perfect guide, with all the answers. There have been many criticisms of this work over the years since 1835, the chief of which are these:

— Tocqueville ignored the economic side of democracy, and failed to assess the importance of the industrial revolution for America.
— In fact, he was more interested in France than the United States. As the English Tories said, his observations were "made from the meridian of Paris," and were therefore distorted pictures of America.
— His method was faulty, and his facts often inaccurate because they were derived from biased sources, in particular from the tiny residue of defeated Federalists.
— He did not emphasize the English influence and tradition in American life sufficiently.
— His terms were not well defined, he was excessively moral and proreligion; he knew too little of America's historical background and made many errors on small points of fact.

All these charges are easily answered and have been rebutted by specialists. For the average intelligent citizen, looking for a better understanding of democracy, and its problematic future, they are simply irrelevant. They refer to Tocqueville as a guide to the past; most of us are interested rather in his many suggestive insights and predictions of the democratic future.

No authority on America has equaled him in prophetic vision. Wilhelm Dilthey called him the greatest historical analyst "since Aristotle and Machiavelli."[31] Patrice Higonnet states that more people of the world have interpreted America "through the prism of

his work than through that of any other writer."[32] Denis Brogan believes that *Democracy in America* continues to be "an admirable
tract for our times," more than a century after its first appearance.[33]

One early American reviewer (1838) declared that for understanding and preserving liberty, "the intelligent American reader
can find no better guide."[34] A recent American scholar (1976) sup-
ports and updates that estimate: "Tocqueville's relevance to the
present, and indeed possibly to the rest of this century, may very
well be greater than it has been ever before."[35]

We who present this little book for your attention, strongly concur
with both judgments.

Tocqueville's Greatest Comments: Some Representative Examples

A few general observations may help to put this taste of Tocqueville—perhaps the reader's first—in more usable perspective. One does not need any special knowledge of American history to understand him; merely some experience with and interest in our present American society and its worries, common to all alert citizens who follow the news and discuss events with friends, is required.

The selections which follow constitute a representative, balanced, introductory sample which should convey a sense of the spirit, insight, and continuing relevance of Tocqueville on America. We hope it will attract many of you to the unabridged main text, all of which is quotable, usable, and good food for reflection.

Most of the selections come from *Democracy in America,* the Phillips Bradley edition, available in paperback in two volumes from Vintage Books, a division of Random House. The remaining quotations are from Tocqueville's "Travel Notes," published as *Journey to America,* by Yale University Press, and from the uncompleted *European Revolution* and the *Correspondence with Gobineau* which were issued as a single volume by Doubleday/Anchor. Excerpts are divided into four sections by general subject matter—economic, political, social, and cultural. A more precise subject index at the end of this book will be helpful in locating quotations of a special interest more easily.

Do Americans feel differently about their country today than 150 years ago when Tocqueville observed us? Here's an illustrative sample, written in 1856 rather than 1831, but on "American Democracy" without reference to Tocqueville. The author, one Joshua Levitt, made two points; you be the judge of how much we have changed since then. "American Democracy claims to be, not the best system that imagination can conceive, but the best method of government that man can administer. And it justifies itself when it is shown to be productive of more good and less evil, than any method of government which can be brought into comparison with it."[36] And "American Democracy is the growth of the soil, and hence can never be learned from books written in other lands, or in ages that are long past. It is as unique as our history. . . ."[37]

Perhaps we can't learn American Democracy entirely from Tocqueville's book, written in France, but it does help our understanding. It is a great book which challenges the reader to make more out of our democratic potential. As Professor Herbert Muller of Indiana University says, "*Democracy in America* is one political classic that I would recommend without reservation to all students, conservative, liberal or radical . . . it not only remains basically as relevant today as in its own day but has become more so in the last generation, for Tocqueville was looking to the future, and we can now appreciate his insights more than his contemporaries could . . . it is both more comprehensive and more penetrating than any contemporary studies I know of."[38]

1

Democracy in the American Economic Substructure

Did Tocqueville appreciate the importance of the industrial revolution in America? Yes, but he was much less interested in industrial growth itself, than he was in the social effects of industrialism, where he showed "amazing prevision." Was he opposed to industrialism? No, because he thought it a democratizing force. However, he was well aware of certain dangers in industrial organization, and the excessive materialism which often accompanied business prosperity. Self-interest he strongly endorsed, "if properly understood." Finally, Tocqueville was no economic determinist like Marx. He believed that man, using his brains, his will to act, and moral sense, was capable of directing society away from the shoals of economic and social disaster.

The Economy: Industry, transportation, and communication

1. The inhabitants of the United States constitute a great civilized people, which fortune has placed in the midst of an uncultivated country, at a distance of three thousand miles from the central point of civilization. America consequently stands in daily need of Europe. The Americans will no doubt ultimately succeed in producing or manufacturing at home most of the articles that they require; but the two continents can never be independent of each other, so numerous are the natural ties between their wants, their ideas, their habits, and their manners.

America needs Europe, since it will never be totally self-sufficient

1:439

2. Americans are constantly driven to engage in commerce and industry. Their origin, their social condi-

**American
Democracy
promotes unusual
activity in
commerce and
industry**

tion, their political institutions, and even the region they
inhabit urge them irresistibly in this direction. Their present condition, then, is that of an almost exclusively manufacturing and commercial association, placed in the
midst of a new and boundless country, which their principal object is to explore for purposes of profit. This is
the characteristic that most distinguishes the American
people from all others at the present time.

2:247–48

**Transportation and
communication—
key to American
economic success**

3. I only know of one means of increasing the prosperity of a people, whose application is infallible and on
which I think one can count in all countries and in all
places.

That means is none other than increasing the facility
of communication between men.

On this point what can be seen in America is both
strange and instructive.

The roads, the canals and the post play a prodigious
part in the prosperity of the Union. It is good to examine
their effects, the value attached to them and the way
they are obtained.

America, which is the country which enjoys the greatest sum of prosperity that has ever yet been vouchsafed
to any nation, is also that which, in proportion to its age
and means, has made the greatest effort to supply itself
with the free communications of which I was speaking
above.

Journey to America, 270

**U.S. development
of efficient,
inexpensive postal
service**

4. In America one of the first things done in a new
State is to make the post go there; in the forests of
Michigan there is no cabin so isolated, no valley so wild
but that letters and newspapers arrive at least once a
week; we have seen that. It is especially in these conditions that I felt the difference between our own French
social state and that of the American people. There are
few rural districts in France in which, proportionately
speaking, as many letters and newspapers are received
as in these still savage lands where man still fights
against all the miseries of life and only has glimpses of
society at long intervals.

Journey to America, 270

5.   Of all the countries in the world America is that in which the spread of ideas and of human industry is most continual and most rapid. There is not an American but knows the resources of all the parts of the vast land that he inhabits; all the able men in the Union know each other by reputation, many of them personally. I have often been struck by astonishment to find how far that is the case. I can say that it has never happened to me to speak to an American about one of his compatriots without finding that he was up-to-date in knowing both how he was now placed and the story of his life.

Economic impact of effective mass education

I know that this intense industrial and intellectual movement is particularly encouraged by education, by the sort of government America enjoys, and by the altogether special situation in which the Americans find themselves.

Journey to America, 271

The Business Dynamic: The principle of self-interest, the work ethic

6.   It is difficult to say for what reason the Americans can navigate at a lower rate than other nations; one is at first led to attribute this superiority to the physical advantages that nature gives them; but it is not so. The American vessels cost almost as much to build as our own; they are not better built, and they generally last a shorter time. The pay of the American sailor is higher than the pay on board European ships, as is proved by the great number of Europeans who are to be found in the merchant vessels of the United States. How does it happen, then, that the Americans sail their vessels at a cheaper rate than we can ours? I am of the opinion that the true cause of their superiority must not be sought for in physical advantages, but that it is wholly attributable to moral and intellectual qualities.

U.S. economic success due less to cheap labor or materials than to moral and intellectual quality of its people

1:441

7.   The whole life of an American is passed like a game of chance, a revolutionary crisis, or a battle.

Americans enjoy competition

1:443

8.   One of the distinguishing characteristics of a democratic period is the taste that all men then have for easy

American desire for material success: Jefferson's "pursuit of happiness"

success and present enjoyment. This occurs in the pursuits of the intellect as well as in all others. Most of those who live in a time of equality are full of an ambition equally alert and indolent: they want to obtain great success immediately, but they would prefer to avoid great effort. These conflicting tendencies lead straight to the search for general ideas, by the aid of which they flatter themselves that they can delineate vast objects with little pains and draw the attention of the public without much trouble.

2:18

Unique American tenderness to the losers in the pursuit of economic happiness

9.   [In the United States] boldness of enterprise is the foremost cause of its rapid progress, its strength, and its greatness. Commercial business is there like a vast lottery, by which a small number of men continually lose, but the state is always a gainer; such a people ought therefore to encourage and do honor to boldness in commercial speculations. But any bold speculation risks the fortune of the speculator and of all those who put their trust in him. The Americans, who make a virtue of commercial temerity, have no right in any case to brand with disgrace those who practice it. Hence arises the strange indulgence that is shown to bankrupts in the United States; their honor does not suffer by such an accident.

2:248–49

The principle of self-interest rightly understood

10.   The Americans, on the other hand, are fond of explaining almost all the actions of their lives by the principle of self-interest rightly understood; they show with complacency how an enlightened regard for themselves constantly prompts them to assist one another and inclines them willingly to sacrifice a portion of their time and property to the welfare of the state. In this respect I think they frequently fail to do themselves justice; for in the United States as well as elsewhere people are sometimes seen to give way to those disinterested and spontaneous impulses that are natural to man; but the Americans seldom admit that they yield to emotions of this kind; they are more anxious to do honor to their philosophy than to themselves.

2:130

11.   The principle of self-interest rightly understood is not a lofty one, but it is clear and sure. It does not aim at mighty objects, but attains without exertion all those at which it aims. As it lies within the reach of all capacities, everyone can without difficulty learn and retain it. By its admirable conformity to human weaknesses it easily obtains great dominion; nor is that dominion precarious, since the principle checks one personal interest by another, and uses, to direct the passions, the very same instrument that excites them.

How self-interest works to motivate Americans

The principle of self-interest rightly understood produces no great acts of self-sacrifice, but it suggests daily small acts of self-denial. By itself it cannot suffice to make a man virtuous; but it disciplines a number of persons in habits of regularity, temperance, moderation, foresight, self-command; and if it does not lead men straight to virtue by the will, it gradually draws them in that direction by their habits. . . .

I am not afraid to say that the principle of self-interest rightly understood appears to me the best suited of all philosophical theories to the wants of the men of our time, and that I regard it as their chief remaining security against themselves. Towards it, therefore, the minds of the moralists of our age should turn; even should they judge it to be incomplete, it must nevertheless be adopted as necessary.

2:131

12.   I do not believe that self-interest is the sole motive of religious men, but I believe that self-interest is the principal means that religions themselves employ to govern men, and I do not question that in this way they strike the multitude and become popular. I do not see clearly why the principle of interest rightly understood should undermine the religious opinions of men; it seems to me more easy to show why it should strengthen them.

How self-interest works in religion

2:134

13.   Among a democratic people, where there is no hereditary wealth, every man works to earn a living, or has worked, or is born of parents who have worked. The notion of labor is therefore presented to the mind,

Work ethic and the dignity of labor

on every side, as the necessary, natural, and honest condition of human existence. Not only is labor not dishonorable among such a people, but it is held in honor; the prejudice is not against it, but in its favor. In the United States a wealthy man thinks that he owes it to public opinion to devote his leisure to some kind of industrial or commercial pursuit or to public business. He would think himself in bad repute if he employed his life solely in living. It is for the purpose of escaping this obligation to work that so many rich Americans come to Europe, where they find some scattered remains of aristocratic society, among whom idleness is still held in honor.

Equality of conditions not only ennobles the notion of labor, but raises the notion of labor as a source of profit.

2:161

Pride in work promotes self-respect

14. This serves to explain the opinions that the Americans entertain with respect to different callings. In America no one is degraded because he works, for everyone about him works also; nor is anyone humiliated by the notion of receiving pay, for the President of the United States also works for pay. He is paid for commanding, other men for obeying orders. In the United States professions are more or less laborious, more or less profitable; but they are never either high or low: every honest calling is honorable.

1:162

Americans dislike and fear laziness and idleness

15. In a democratic society like that of the United States, where fortunes are scanty and insecure, everybody works, and work opens a way to everything; this has changed the point of honor quite around and has turned it against idleness.

2:250

Effect of democracy on the work ethic

16. Thus, democracy not only swells the number of working-men, but leads men to prefer one kind of labor to another; and while it diverts them from agriculture, it encourages their tastes for commerce and manufactures.

2:163–64

17. A similar observation is likewise applicable to all men living in democracies, whether they are poor or rich. Those who live in the midst of democratic fluctuations have always before their eyes the image of chance; and they end by liking all undertakings in which chance plays a part. They are therefore all led to engage in commerce, not only for the sake of the profit it holds out to them, but for the love of the constant excitement occasioned by that pursuit.

"Enterprise": The spirit of work as a game

2:165

18. *Everyone has an equal right to work.* Is this not a new maxim, quite different from that of Christ, who said, after Moses: *Man is condemned to work?* What used to be a painful duty becomes a right, a prerogative in the name of which each member of the social body has the right not to suffer from misery and destitution. The power and dignity which morality has gained by this principle are beyond question.

The right to work as a liberating force

Correspondence with Gobineau, 200

Affluence and Its Effects: The quality of life, materialism

19. Among a nation where aristocracy predominates in society and keeps it stationary, the people in the end get as much accustomed to poverty as the rich to their opulence. . . .

The taste for material comfort— natural and strongest in the middle class

When, on the contrary, the distinctions of ranks are obliterated and privileges are destroyed, when hereditary property is subdivided and education and freedom are widely diffused, the desire of acquiring the comforts of the world haunts the imagination of the poor, and the dread of losing them that of the rich. . . .

If I were to inquire what passion is most natural to men who are stimulated and circumscribed by the obscurity of their birth or the mediocrity of their fortune, I could discover none more peculiarly appropriate to their condition than this love of physical prosperity. The passion for physical comforts is essentially a passion of the middle classes; with those classes it grows and spreads, with them it is preponderant. From them it

mounts into the higher orders of society and descends
into the mass of the people.

2:137

Taste for material comforts: another aspect of the "pursuit of happiness"

20.   The taste for physical gratifications leads a democratic people into no such excesses. The love of well-
being is there displayed as a tenacious, exclusive, universal passion, but its range is confined. To build
enormous palaces, to conquer or to mimic nature, to
ransack the world in order to gratify the passions of a
man, is not thought of, but to add a few yards of land to
your field, to plant an orchard, or enlarge a dwelling, to
be always making life more comfortable and convenient, to avoid trouble, and to satisfy the smallest wants
without effort and almost without cost. These are small
objects, but the soul clings to them; it dwells upon them
closely and day by day, till they at last shut out the rest
of the world and sometimes intervene between itself
and heaven.

2:140

Effect of egalitarianism on the materialistic urge

21.   But men will never establish any equality with
which they can be contented. Whatever efforts a people
may make, they will never succeed in reducing all the
conditions of society to a perfect level; and even if they
unhappily attained that absolute and complete equality
of position, the inequality of minds would still remain,
which, coming directly from the hand of God, will forever escape the laws of man.

2:146

Excessive materialism as a threat to good citizenship

22.   There is, indeed, a most dangerous passage in the
history of a democratic people. When the taste for physical gratifications among them has grown more rapidly
than their education and their experience of free institutions, the time will come when men are carried away
and lose all self-restraint at the sight of the new possessions they are about to obtain. In their intense and exclusive anxiety to make a fortune they lose sight of the
close connection that exists between the private fortune
of each and the prosperity of all. It is not necessary to do
violence to such a people in order to strip them of the
rights they enjoy; they themselves willingly loosen their

hold. The discharge of political duties appears to them to be a troublesome impediment which diverts them from their occupations and business. If they are required to elect representatives, to support the government by personal service, to meet on public business, they think they have no time, they cannot waste their precious hours in useless engagements; such idle amusements are unsuited to serious men who are engaged with the more important interest of life. These people think they are following the principle of self-interest, but the idea they entertain of that principle is a very crude one; and the better to look after what they call their own business, they neglect their chief business, which is to remain their own masters.

2:149

23. In democratic countries, where money does not lead those who possess it to political power, but often removes them from it, the rich do not know how to spend their leisure.

2:164–65

Effect of democracy and the work ethic on leisure

24. *Christianity* severely restrained the *passions.* The *present* concept of morality is *indulgent towards them;* it does not renounce the hope to rationalize them since it believes that many of these passions are potentially useful. Thus the love of luxury and of material enjoyments is no longer an evil. To the contrary, if a man works more because he desires to raise his well-being, the urge of well-being in this case becomes a commendable virtue in itself. One may go further to say that any kind of reasonable satisfaction that does, in fact, involve no inconvenience to others is in no way opposed to the morality adopted by our age.

Correspondence with Gobineau, 202

Love of material comforts no longer considered sinful

Future Problems: Class conflict and other dangers

25. I readily admit that public tranquillity is a great good, but at the same time I cannot forget that all nations have been enslaved by being kept in good order. Certainly it is not to be inferred that nations ought to de-

Limits to preservation of order as a social solution

spise public tranquillity, but that state ought not to content them. A nation that asks nothing of its government but the maintenance of order is already a slave at heart, the slave of its own well-being, awaiting only the hand that will bind it.

2:150

Democratic capitalism: Is there an aristocracy of manufacturing in the United States?

26.   The territorial aristocracy of former ages was either bound by law, or thought itself bound by usage, to come to the relief of its serving-men and to relieve their distresses. But the manufacturing aristocracy of our age first impoverishes and debases the men who serve it and then abandons them to be supported by the charity of the public. This is a natural consequence of what has been said before. Between the workman and the master there are frequent relations but no real association.

I am of the opinion, on the whole, that the manufacturing aristocracy which is growing up under our eyes is one of the harshest that ever existed in the world; but at the same time it is one of the most confined and least dangerous. Nevertheless, the friends of democracy should keep their eyes anxiously fixed in this direction; for if ever a permanent inequality of conditions and aristocracy again penetrates into the world, it may be predicted that this is the gate by which they will enter.

2:171

How democracy softens the spirit of class conflict

27.   As servants do not form a separate class, they have no habits, prejudices, or manners peculiar to themselves; they are not remarkable for any particular turn of mind or moods of feeling. They know no vices or virtues of their condition, but they partake of the education, the opinions, the feelings, the virtues, and the vices of their contemporaries; and they are honest men or scoundrels in the same way as their masters are. . . .

In democracies servants are not only equal among themselves, but it may be said that they are, in some sort, the equals of their masters. This requires explanation in order to be rightly understood. At any moment a servant may become a master, and he aspires to rise to that condition; the servant is therefore not a different man from the master.

2:191

28. In democracies the condition of domestic service does not degrade the character of those who enter upon it, because it is freely chosen and adopted for a time only, because it is not stigmatized by public opinion and creates no permanent inequality between the servant and the master.

How democracy gives dignity to domestic workers

2:194

29. Most of the remarks that I have already made in speaking of masters and servants may be applied to masters and workmen. As the gradations of the social scale come to be less observed, while the great sink and the humble rise and poverty as well as opulence ceases to be hereditary, the distance, both in reality and in opinion, which heretofore separated the workman from the master is lessened every day. The workman conceives a more lofty opinion of his rights, of his future, of himself; he is filled with new ambition and new desires, he is harassed by new wants. Every instant he views with longing eyes the profits of his employer; and in order to share them he strives to dispose of his labor at a higher rate, and he generally succeeds at length in the attempt.

How democracy gives hope and dignity to the industrial laborer

2:199

30. I think that, on the whole, it may be asserted that a slow and gradual rise of wages is one of the general laws of democratic communities. In proportion as social conditions become more equal, wages rise; and as wages are higher, social conditions become more equal.

Wages tend to rise in a democracy

2:200

31. I believe that ambitious men in democracies are less engrossed than any others with the interests and the judgment of posterity; the present moment alone engages and absorbs them. They are more apt to complete a number of undertakings with rapidity than to raise lasting monuments of their achievements, and they care much more for success than for fame.

Business enterprise usually prefers success to fame, lessening its interest in the long-range future

2:261

32. I confess that I apprehend much less for democratic society from the boldness than from the mediocri-

One danger in democracies: Business success can lead to loss of initiative and mediocrity

ty of desires. What appears to me most to be dreaded is that in the midst of the small, incessant occupations of private life, ambition should lose its vigor and its greatness; that the passions of man should abate, but at the same time be lowered; so that the march of society should every day become more tranquil and less aspiring.

I think, then, that the leaders of modern society would be wrong to seek to lull the community by a state of too uniform and too peaceful happiness, and that it is well to expose it from time to time to matters of difficulty and danger in order to raise ambition and to give it a field of action.

2:261

European experience suggests that industrial growth arouses public fear and attracts government regulation

33.   There exists among the modern nations of Europe one great cause, independent of all those which have already been pointed out, which perpetually contributes to extend the agency or to strengthen the prerogative of the supreme power, though it has not been sufficiently attended to: I mean the growth of manufactures, which is fostered by the progress of social equality. Manufacturers generally collect a multitude of men on the same spot, among whom new and complex relations spring up. These men are exposed by their calling to great and sudden alternations of plenty and want, during which public tranquillity is endangered. It may also happen that these employments sacrifice the health and even the life of those who gain by them or of those who live by them. Thus, the manufacturing classes require more regulation, superintendence, and restraint than the other classes of society, and it is natural that the powers of government should increase in the same proportion as those classes.

2:327

2

Democracy as a Political System: American Style

Tocqueville visited America at a time when democratic government had reached an all-time high of popularity. Democratic institutions were believed to be the assured key to total success for a society—with democracy all social, economic, and cultural problems would fall into place and quickly solve themselves. Most people knew that our revolution was of the political variety, not a social revolution like the one in France. Yet, all over Europe the United States had an ill-deserved reputation for extreme radicalism. This was because we had rejected decent monarchy for dangerous republicanism, replacing decent aristocracy with untested representative democracy and putting our faith in a new written Constitution rather than unwritten customs and traditions.

The young French visitor was interested in democracy, naturally, but in equality a great deal more. As a Frenchman, he had plenty of direct experience with the democratic trio of *liberté, égalité,* and *fraternité,* and knew how hard it was to make them all work well at the same time. Equality was the really upsetting principle. At this date, equality was being demanded everywhere, but applied extensively only in America. So although Tocqueville had to give primary attention to democratic political institutions in the United States, he did so with all kinds of social angles, accents, and speculations.

Tocqueville believed in checks and balances. He worried about too much democracy (tyranny of the majority), too much equality (homogenization), too much centralization (loss of individual liberty) and a general decline of excellence. The organization of these comments on American political arrangements is intended to make Tocqueville's major emphases a little clearer.

The Constitution and Associated Democratic Machinery

Underlying principles of a democracy

1. In America the principle of the sovereignty of the people is neither barren nor concealed, as it is with some other nations; it is recognized by the customs and proclaimed by the laws; it spreads freely, and arrives without impediment at its most remote consequences. If there is a country in the world where the doctrine of the sovereignty of the people can be fairly appreciated, where it can be studied in its application to the affairs of society, and where its dangers and its advantages may be judged, that country is assuredly America.

1:57

Basis of democratic government: Vigorous local governing system

2. Yet municipal institutions constitute the strength of free nations. Town meetings are to liberty what primary schools are to science; they bring it within the people's reach, they teach men how to use and how to enjoy it. A nation may establish a free government, but without municipal institutions it cannot have the spirit of liberty.

1:63

Democratic government in United States quite effective

3. In America the power that conducts the administration is far less regular, less enlightened, and less skillful, but a hundredfold greater than in Europe. In no country in the world do the citizens make such exertions for the common weal. I know of no people who have established schools so numerous and efficacious, places of public worship better suited to the wants of the inhabitants, or roads kept in better repair.

1:95

Judicial organization difficult to understand

4. Confederations have existed in other countries besides America; I have seen republics elsewhere than upon the shores of the New World alone: the representative system of government has been adopted in several states of Europe; but I am not aware that any nation of the globe has hitherto organized a judicial power in the same manner as the Americans. The judicial organization of the United States is the institution which a stranger has the greatest difficulty understanding.

1:102

5. The public spirit of the Union is, so to speak, noth-   **Sources of**
ing more than an aggregate or summary of the patriotic   **national patriotic**
zeal of the separate provinces. Every citizen of the Unit-   **sentiment**
ed States transfers, so to speak, his attachment to his little republic into the common store of American patriotism. In defending the Union he defends the increasing
prosperity of his own state or county, the right of con-
ducting its affairs, and the hope of causing measures of
improvement to be adopted in it which may be favorable to his own interests; and these are motives that are
wont to stir men more than the general interests of the
country and the glory of the nation.

1:170

6. In examining the Constitution of the United   **Opinion of**
States, which is the most perfect federal constitution that   **American**
ever existed, one is startled at the variety of information   **Constitution**
and the amount of discernment that it presupposes in
the people whom it is meant to govern. The government of the Union depends almost entirely upon legal
fictions; the Union is an ideal nation, which exists, so to
speak, only in the mind, and whose limits and extent
can only be discerned by the understanding.

1:172

Democracy: Good and bad aspects; possibility of a tyranny of the majority

7. Long and patient observation and much acquired   **Masses have**
knowledge are requisite to form a just estimate of the   **trouble**
character of a single individual. Men of the greatest gen-   **recognizing true**
ius often fail to do it, and can it be supposed that the   **leaders**
common people will always succeed? The people have
neither the time nor the means for an investigation of
this kind. Their conclusions are hastily formed from a
superficial inspection of the more prominent features of
a question. Hence it often happens that mountebanks
of all sorts are able to please the people, while their
truest friends frequently fail to gain their confidence.

1:208

Why democracies are chronically spendthrift

8.   Let us now suppose that the legislative authority is vested in the lowest order: there are two striking reasons which show that the tendency of the expenditures will be to increase, not to diminish.

As the great majority of those who create the laws have no taxable property, all the money that is spent for the community appears to be spent to their advantage, at no cost of their own; and those who have some little property readily find means of so regulating the taxes that they weigh upon the wealthy and profit the poor, although the rich cannot take the same advantage when they are in possession of the government.

In countries in which the poor have the exclusive power of making the laws, no great economy of public expenditure ought to be expected; that expenditure will always be considerable, either because the taxes cannot weigh upon those who levy them, or because they are levied in such a manner as not to reach these poorer classes. In other words, the government of the democracy is the only one under which the power that votes the taxes escapes the payment of them.

1:221–22

Democracy weak in preparing for future

9.   But it is this clear perception of the future, founded upon judgment and experience, that is frequently wanting in democracies. The people are more apt to feel than to reason. . . .

1:237

Legislative turmoil: its significance

10.   The great political agitation of American legislative bodies, which is the only one that attracts the attention of foreigners, is a mere episode, or a sort of continuation, of that universal movement which originates in the lowest classes of the people and extends successively to all the ranks of society. It is impossible to spend more effort in the pursuit of happiness.

1:259

Election clamor: its significance

11.   This ceaseless agitation which democratic government has introduced into the political world influences all social intercourse. I am not sure that, on the whole, this is not the greatest advantage of democracy; and I

am less inclined to applaud it for what it does than for what it causes to be done.

It is incontestable that the people frequently conduct public business very badly; but it is impossible that the lower orders should take a part in public business without extending the circle of their ideas and quitting the ordinary routine of their thoughts. The humblest individual who cooperates in the government of society acquires a certain degree of self-respect . . .

1:260

12. . . . I am firmly convinced that the democratic revolution which we are now beholding is an irresistible fact, against which it would be neither desirable nor prudent to contend, . . .

Spread of democracy is inevitable

2:vi

13. Hence it is that in democratic countries parties are so impatient of control and are never manageable except in moments of great public danger. Even then the authority of leaders, which under such circumstances may be able to make men act or speak, hardly ever reaches the extent of making them keep silence.

Political parties in democracies lack discipline

2:94

14. There is hardly a member of Congress who can make up his mind to go home without having dispatched at least one speech to his constituents. . . .

Congressmen love to talk

2:97

15. I can conceive nothing more admirable or more powerful than a great orator debating great questions of state in a democratic assembly.

Yet some talk is admirable

2:98

16. From a general, higher viewpoint patriotism, despite its great impulses and deeds, would seem a false and narrow passion. The great efforts suggested by patriotism are, in reality, due to humanity and not to those small fragments of the human race within particular limits called peoples or nations. It would seem, at first sight, that those Christian moralists especially who are in-

Why patriotism is justifiable

clined to care more for humanity than for their father-
land are right. . . .

Man has been created by God (I do not know why) in
such a way that the larger the object of his love the less
directly attached he is to it. His heart needs particular
passions; he needs limited objects for his affections to
keep these firm and enduring. There are but few who
will burn with ardent love for the entire human species
. . . I am convinced that the interests of the human race
are better served by giving every man a particular fa-
therland than by trying to inflame his passions for the
whole of humanity. [Which] the common man will perceive only from a viewpoint that is distant, aloof, . . .
and cold.

European Revolution, 169–70

**Tyranny of the
majority**

17.   In my opinion, the main evil of the present democratic institutions of the United States does not arise, as
is often asserted in Europe, from their weakness, but
from their irresistible strength. I am not so much
alarmed at the excessive liberty which reigns in that
country as at the inadequate securities which one finds
there against tyranny.

When an individual or a party is wronged in the United States, to whom can he apply for redress? If to public
opinion, public opinion constitutes the majority; if to the
legislature, it represents the majority and implicitly
obeys it; if to the executive power, it is appointed by the
majority and serves as a passive tool in its hands. The
public force consists of the majority under arms; the jury
is the majority invested with the right of hearing judicial
cases; and in certain states even the judges are elected
by the majority. However iniquitous or absurd the
measure of which you complain, you must submit to it
as well as you can.

1:270–71

**Effect on quality of
leadership**

18.   I attribute the small number of distinguished men
in political life to the ever increasing despotism of the
majority in the United States.

1:276

19.   If ever the free institutions of America are destroyed, that event may be attributed to the omnipo-

tence of the majority, which may at some future time
urge the minorities to desperation and oblige them to
have recourse to physical force. Anarchy will then be
the result, but it will have been brought about by despotism.

**A possible threat
to individual
liberties.**

1:279

20.   I think, then, that the species of oppression by
which democratic nations are menaced is unlike anything that ever before existed in the world; our contemporaries will find no prototype of it in their memories. I
seek in vain for an expression that will accurately convey the whole of the idea I have formed of it: the old
words *despotism* and *tyranny* are inappropriate: the
thing itself is new, and since I cannot name, I must attempt to define it.

**Classic statement
on the nature of
democratic
despotism**

I seek to trace the novel features under which despotism may appear in the world. The first thing that strikes
the observation is an innumerable multitude of men, all
equal and alike, incessantly endeavoring to procure the
petty and paltry pleasures with which they glut their
lives. Each of them, living apart, is as a stranger to the
fate of all the rest; his children and his private friends
constitute to him the whole of mankind. As for the rest
of his fellow citizens, he is close to them, but does not
see them; he touches them, but he does not feel them;
he exists only in himself and for himself alone; and if his
kindred still remain to him, he may be said at any rate to
have lost his country.

Above this race of men stands an immense and tute-
lary power, which takes upon itself alone to secure their
gratifications and to watch over their fate. That power is
absolute, minute, regular, provident, and mild. It would
be like the authority of a parent if, like that authority, its
object was to prepare men for manhood; but it seeks,
on the contrary, to keep them in perpetual childhood: it
is well content that the people should rejoice, provided
they think of nothing but rejoicing. For their happiness
such a government willingly labors, but it chooses to be
the sole agent and the only arbiter of that happiness; it
provides for their security, foresees and supplies their
necessities, facilitates their pleasures, manages their
principal concerns, directs their industry, regulates the

**When democratic
bureaucracy
becomes a
benevolent despot**

descent of property, and subdivides their inheritances:
what remains, but to spare them all the care of thinking
and all the trouble of living?

2:336

The pattern of
bureaucracy in
democratic
despotism

21.   After having thus successively taken each member
of the community in its powerful grasp and fashioned
him at will, the supreme power then extends its arm
over the whole community. It covers the surface of society with a network of small complicated rules, minute
and uniform, through which the most original minds
and the most energic characters cannot penetrate, to
rise above the crowd. The will of man is not shattered,
but softened, bent, and guided; men are seldom forced
by it to act, but they are constantly restrained from acting. Such a power does not destroy, but it prevents existence; it does not tyrannize, but it compresses, ener-
vates, extinguishes, and stupefies a people, till each
nation is reduced to nothing better than a flock of timid
and industrious animals, of which the government is the
shepherd.

2:337

Democratic
ambiguity

22.   Our contemporaries are constantly excited by two
conflicting passions: they want to be led, and they wish
to remain free.

2:337

Public taste for
administrative
despotism plus
popular
sovereignty

23.   By this system the people shake off their state of
dependence just long enough to select their master and
then relapse into it again. A great many persons at the
present day are quite contented with this sort of compromise between administrative despotism and the sovereignty of the people; and they think they have done
enough for the protection of individual freedom when
they have surrendered it to the power of the nation at
large. This does not satisfy me: the nature of him I am to
obey signifies less to me than the fact of extorted obedience.

2:337–38

24.   It must not be forgotten that it is especially dangerous to enslave men in the minor details of life. For my

own part, I should be inclined to think freedom less necessary in great things than in little ones, if it were possible to be secure of the one without possessing the other.
2:338

Enslavement is worst when it governs the small details of life

25. I believe that it is easier to establish an absolute and despotic government among a people in which the conditions of society are equal than among any other; and I think that if such a government were once established among such a people, it not only would oppress men, but would eventually strip each of them of several of the highest qualities of humanity. Despotism, therefore, appears to me peculiarly to be dreaded in democratic times. I should have loved freedom, I believe, at all times, but in the time in which we live I am ready to worship it.
2:340

Democracy is the easiest form of government to "despotize"

26. The socialists have produced, and are still producing, so much fear that even the corner grocer does not want to hear anything discussed that is unorthodox; he keeps repeating that the people should be kept within bounds to impede the abolition of Property and Family, and to prevent them from ransacking his grocery. There is now little taste for freedom of thought; it is enough for an idea to seem dangerous and a sort of universal silence is drawn around it. There is not enough faith, not enough passion, not enough vitality to combat such ideas; instead they are shunned, passed over in silence, neither rejected nor recognized.
Correspondence with Gobineau, 224–25

Socialism is no friend of freedom of thought

27. ... For democratic nations to be virtuous and prosperous, they require but to will it.
2:352

Healthy democracy must preserve the will to act

28. You consider people today as if they were overgrown children, very degenerate and very ill-educated. And, consequently, it seems proper to you that they should be led with blinds, through noise, with a great clangor of bells, in nicely embroidered uniforms, which are often but liveries of servants. I, too, believe that our contemporaries have been badly brought up and that

Healthy democracy requires faith in one's fellow citizens

this is a prime cause of their miseries and of their weakness, but I believe that a better upbringing could repair the wrongs done by their miseducation; I believe that it is not permissible to renounce such an effort. I believe that one could still achieve something with our contemporaries, as with all men, through an able appeal to their natural decency and common sense. In brief, I wish to treat them like human beings. Maybe I am wrong. But I am merely following the consequences of my principles and, moreover, I find a deep and inspiring pleasure in following them. You profoundly distrust mankind, at least our kind; you believe that it is not only decadent but incapable of ever lifting itself up again. . . . To me, human societies, like persons, become something worth while only through their use of liberty. I have always said that it is more difficult to stabilize and to maintain liberty in our new democratic societies than in certain aristocratic societies of the past. But I shall never dare to think it impossible. And I pray to God lest He inspire me with the idea that one might as well despair of trying. No, I shall not believe that this human race, which is at the head of all visible creation, has become that bastardized flock of sheep which you say it is.

Correspondence with Gobineau, 309–10

Equality and Individualism: Do they threaten liberty?

Individualism and self-reliance

29.   Hence arises the maxim, that everyone is the best and sole judge of his own private interest, and that society has no right to control a man's actions unless they are prejudicial to the common weal or unless the common weal demands his help. This doctrine is universally admitted in the United States.

1:67

Democracy fosters a "passion for equality"

30.   Democratic institutions awaken and foster a passion for equality which they can never entirely satisfy. This complete equality eludes the grasp of the people at the very moment when they think they have grasped it, and "flies," as Pascal says, "with an eternal flight"; the people are excited in the pursuit of an advantage, which is more precious because it is not sufficiently re-

mote to be unknown or sufficiently near to be enjoyed. The lower orders are agitated by the chance of success, they are irritated by its uncertainty; and they pass from the enthusiasm of pursuit to the exhaustion of ill success, and lastly to the acrimony of disappointment. Whatever transcends their own limitations appears to be an obstacle to their desires, and there is no superiority, however legitimate it may be, which is not irksome in their sight.

1:208

31. Although men cannot become absolutely equal unless they are entirely free, and consequently equality, pushed to its furthest extent, may be confounded with freedom, yet there is good reason for distinguishing the one from the other. The taste which men have for liberty and that which they feel for equality are, in fact, two different things; and I am not afraid to add that among democratic nations they are two unequal things.

Liberty and equality are not the same thing

2:100

32. Political liberty bestows exalted pleasures from time to time upon a certain number of citizens. Equality every day confers a number of small enjoyments on every man. The charms of equality are every instant felt and are within the reach of all; the noblest hearts are not insensible to them and the most vulgar souls exult in them. The passion that equality creates must therefore be at once strong and general. Men cannot enjoy political liberty unpurchased by some sacrifices, and they never obtain it without great exertions. But the pleasures of equality are self-proffered; each of the petty incidents of life seems to occasion them, and in order to taste them, nothing is required but to live.

Liberty requires sacrifice; equality doesn't

2:101–02

33. Selfishness blights the germ of all virtue; individualism, at first, only saps the virtues of public life; but in the long run it attacks and destroys all others and is at length absorbed in downright selfishness. Selfishness is a vice as old as the world, which does not belong to one form of society more than to another; individualism is of

Close relation of liberty, individualism, and selfishness

democratic origin and it threatens to spread in the same
ratio as the equality of condition.

2:104

Americans born
equal

34.   The great advantage of the Americans is that they
have arrived at a state of democracy without having to
endure a democratic revolution, and that they are born
equal instead of becoming so.

2:108

Individualism and
good citizenship

35.   It is difficult to draw a man out of his own circle to
interest him in the destiny of the state, because he does
not clearly understand what influence the destiny of the
state can have upon his own lot. But if it is proposed to
make a road cross the end of his estate, he will see at a
glance that there is a connection between this small
public affair and his greatest private affairs; and he will
discover, without its being shown to him, the close tie
that unites private to general interest. Thus far more
may be done by entrusting to the citizens the administration of minor affairs than by surrendering to them in
the control of important ones, towards interesting them
in the public welfare and convincing them that they constantly stand in need of one another in order to provide
for it.

2:111

Individualism and
public welfare

36.   It would be unjust to suppose that the patriotism
and the zeal that every American displays for the welfare
of his fellow citizens are wholly insincere. Although private interest directs the greater part of human actions in
the United States as well as elsewhere, it does not regulate them all. I must say that I have often seen Americans make great and real sacrifices to the public welfare;
and I have noticed a hundred instances in which they
hardly ever failed to lend faithful support to one another. The free institutions which the inhabitants of the
United States possess, and the political rights of which
they make so much use, remind every citizen, and in a
thousand ways, that he lives in society. . . .

Men attend to the interests of the public, first by necessity, afterwards by choice; what was intentional becomes an instinct, and by dint of working for the good of

one's fellow citizens, the habit and the taste for serving them are at length acquired.

2:112

37.   In democratic ages men rarely sacrifice themselves for one another, but they display general compassion for the members of the human race. They inflict no useless ills, and they are happy to relieve the griefs of others when they can do so without much hurting themselves; they are not disinterested, but they are humane.

Equality and compassion

Although the Americans have in a manner reduced selfishness to a social and philosophical theory, they are nevertheless extremely open to compassion. In no country is criminal justice administered with more mildness than in the United States.

2:176

38.   On the contrary, in proportion as nations become more like each other, they become reciprocally more compassionate, and the law of nations is mitigated.

Effect of equality on laws of nations

2:177

39.   In a foreign country two Americans are at once friends simply because they are Americans. They are repulsed by no prejudice; they are attracted by their common country. For two Englishmen the same blood is not enough; they must be brought together by the same rank.

Equality promotes national fraternity

2:180

40.   The temper of the Americans is vindictive, like that of all serious and reflecting nations. They hardly ever forget an offense, but it is not easy to offend them, and their resentment is as slow to kindle as it is to abate.

Equality promotes national sensitivity

2:181

41.   When men feel a natural compassion for the sufferings of one another, when they are brought together by easy and frequent intercourse, and no sensitive feelings keep them asunder, it may readily be supposed that they will lend assistance to one another whenever it is needed. When an American asks for the co-operation of his fellow citizens, it is seldom refused; and I have often

Equality fosters social sensitivity

seen it afforded spontaneously, and with great goodwill. If an accident happens on the highway, everybody hastens to help the sufferer; if some great and sudden calamity befalls a family, the purses of a thousand strangers are at once willingly opened and small but numerous donations pour in to relieve their distress.

2:185

Equality produces trust in wisdom of public opinion

42. The nearer the people are drawn to the common level of an equal and similar condition, the less prone does each man become to place implicit faith in a certain man or a certain class of men. But his readiness to believe the multitude increases, and opinion is more than ever mistress of the world. Not only is common opinion the only guide which private judgment retains among a democratic people, but among such a people it possesses a power infinitely beyond what it has elsewhere. At periods of equality men have no faith in one another, by reason of their common resemblance; but this very resemblance gives them almost unbounded confidence in the judgment of the public; for it would seem probable that, as they are all endowed with equal means of judging, the greater truth should go with the greater number. . . .

The public, therefore, among a democratic people, has a singular power, which aristocratic nations cannot conceive; for it does not persuade others to its beliefs, but it imposes them and makes them permeate the thinking of everyone by a sort of enormous pressure of the mind of all upon the individual intelligence.

2:11

Equality fairly recent in America

43. Thus among the Americans it is freedom that is old; equality is of comparatively modern date.

2:315

Legal preservation of civil liberties a "must"

44. It is therefore most especially in the present democratic times, that the true friends of the liberty and the greatness of man ought constantly to be on the alert to prevent the power of government from lightly sacrificing the private rights of individuals to the general execution of its designs.

2:345

45. To lay down extensive but distinct and settled limits to the action of the government; to confer certain rights on private persons, and to secure to them the undisputed enjoyment of those rights; to enable individual man to maintain whatever independence, strength, and original power he still possesses; to raise him by the side of society at large, and uphold him in that position; these appear to me the main objects of legislators in the ages upon which we are now entering.

Main objective of legislators should be to protect individual rights

2:347

46. You will see tranquil and prosperous peoples amidst free institutions. They grow, they become rich, they shine. Do not then believe that their independence will endure if it is only these material goods which attach them to liberty. . . .

Enjoyment of freedom attaches people to their rights

Material interest will never be sufficiently permanent and tangible to maintain the love of liberty in the hearts of men unless their taste for it exists. . . .

There is, thus, an intellectual interest in liberty, the main source of which is the tangible benefices which it provides. It is a taste which, it is true, all men have in some way or another; but its primacy exists only in the hearts of very few . . . It is the common source not only of political liberty but of all of the high and manly virtues. . . . It is not so much the material advantages provided but the enjoyment of freedom which attaches free people strongly and jealously to their rights.

The European Revolution, 167–68

47. Another principle of American society, which one must always keep in mind is this: since every individual is the best judge of his own interest, society must not protect him too carefully, lest he should come to rely on it and so saddle society with a task it cannot perform.

Reliance on protection of society fosters impossible expectations of that society

Journey to America, 18

Centralization in Democracy: An irresistible and menacing trend?

48. It is evident that a centralized government acquires immense power when united to centralized administration. Thus combined, it accustoms men to set their own

**Dangers of
centralized
government and
centralized
administration**

will habitually and completely aside; to submit, not only
for once, or upon one point, but in every respect, and at
all times. Not only, therefore, does this union of power
subdue them compulsorily, but it affects their ordinary
habits; it isolates them and then influences each separately.

These two kinds of centralization assist and attract
each other, but they must not be supposed to be insepa-
rable.

1:90

**American versus
French view of
centralization**

49. The partisans of centralization in Europe are wont
to maintain that the government can administer the affairs of each locality better than the citizens can do it for
themselves. This may be true when the central power is
enlightened and the local authorities are ignorant; when
it is alert and they are slow; when it is accustomed to act
and they to obey. Indeed, it is evident that this double
tendency must augment with the increase of centralization, and that the readiness of the one and the incapaci-
ty of the others must become more and more prominent. But I deny that it is so when the people are as
enlightened, as awake to their interests, and as accustomed to reflect on them as the Americans are. I am
persuaded, on the contrary, that in this case the collective strength of the citizens will always conduce more effi-
caciously to the public welfare than the authority of the
government.

1:93

**Political effects of
decentralization
admirable**

50. It is not the *administrative*, but the *political* effects
of decentralization that I most admire in America. In the
United States the interests of the country are everywhere kept in view; they are an object of solicitude to
the people of the whole Union, and every citizen is as
warmly attached to them as if they were his own. He
takes pride in the glory of his nation; he boasts of its success, to which he conceives himself to have contributed;
and he rejoices in the general prosperity by which he
profits. The feeling he entertains towards the state is
analogous to that which unites him to his family, and it is
by a kind of selfishness that he interests himself in the
welfare of his country.

1:98

51.   Small nations have therefore always been the cra-   **Liberty safest in**
dle of political liberty; and the fact that many of them   **small nations**
have lost their liberty by becoming larger shows that
their freedom was more a consequence of their small
size than of the character of the people.

1:166

52.   In democratic communities nothing but the central   **General trend to**
power has any stability in its position or any perma-   **centralization in**
nence in its undertakings. All the citizens are in ceaseless   **democracies**
stir and transformation. Now, it is in the nature of all
governments to seek constantly to enlarge their sphere
of action; hence it is almost impossible that such a government should not ultimately succeed, because it acts
with a fixed principle and a constant will upon men
whose position, ideas, and desires are constantly
changing.

It frequently happens that the members of the community promote the influence of the central power without intending to. Democratic eras are periods of experiment, innovation, and adventure. There is always a
multitude of men engaged in difficult or novel undertakings, which they follow by themselves without shackling
themselves to their fellows. Such persons will admit, as a
general principle, that the public authority ought not to
interfere in private concerns; but, by an exception to
that rule, each of them craves its assistance in the particular concern on which he is engaged and seeks to draw
upon the influence of the government for his own benefit, although he would restrict it on all other occasions. If
a large number of men applies this particular exception
to a great variety of different purposes, the sphere of the
central power extends itself imperceptibly in all directions, although everyone wishes it to be circumscribed.

Thus a democratic government increases its power   **How democratic**
simply by the fact of its permanence. Time is on its side;   **government**
every incident befriends it; the passions of individuals   **increases its**
unconsciously promote it; and it may be asserted that   **power.**
the older a democratic community is, the more centralized will its government become.

2:311–12

Aversion to privileges aids centralization

53.   This never dying, ever kindling hatred which sets a democratic people against the smallest privileges is peculiarly favorable to the gradual concentration of all political rights in the hands of the representative of the state alone.

2:312

Central government, therefore, encourages equality to secure its own role

54.   Every central power, which follows its natural tendencies, courts and encourages the principle of equality; for equality singularly facilitates, extends, and secures the influence of a central power.

2:312

55.   Democratic nations often hate those in whose hands the central power is vested, but they always love that power itself.

2:313

Knowledge checks centralization; ignorance accelerates it

56.   If education enables men at all times to defend their independence, this is most especially true in democratic times. When all men are alike, it is easy to found a sole and all-powerful government by the aid of mere instinct. But men require much intelligence, knowledge, and art to organize and to maintain secondary powers under similar circumstances and to create, amid the independence and individual weakness of the citizens, such free associations as may be able to struggle against tyranny without destroying public order.

Hence the concentration of power and the subjection of individuals will increase among democratic nations, not only in the same proportion as their equality, but in the same proportion as their ignorance.

2:316–17

Democracy tends to sacrifice liberty to security

57.   I have shown how the dread of disturbance and the love of well-being insensibly lead democratic nations to increase the functions of central government as the only power which appears to be intrinsically sufficiently strong, enlightened, and secure to protect them from anarchy, I would now add that all the particular circumstances which tend to make the state of a democratic community agitated and precarious enhance this gener-

al propensity and lead private persons more and more to sacrifice their rights to their tranquility.

2:318

58.　On the other hand, in proportion as the power of a state increases and its necessities are augmented, the state consumption of manufactured produce is always growing larger; and these commodities are generally made in the arsenals or establishments of the government. Thus in every kingdom the ruler becomes the principal manufacturer: he collects and retains in his service a vast number of engineers, architects, mechanics, and handicraftsmen.

Centralized governments are big consumers

2:329

59.　Local liberties may exist for some time without general liberties when such local liberties are traditional, habitual, customary, rooted in memories; or, on the other hand, when despotism is relatively new. But it is senseless to believe that while general liberties are suppressed such local liberties can be voluntarily created.

Local liberties do not last long without national liberties

The European Revolution, 170

Wars and the Military: How they affect democracy uniquely

60.　War is nevertheless an occurrence to which all nations are subject, democratic nations as well as others. Whatever taste they may have for peace, they must hold themselves in readiness to repel aggression. . . .

Democracies must be ready to repel aggression

2:279

61.　In democratic armies the desire of advancement is almost universal: it is ardent, tenacious, perpetual; it is strengthened by all other desires and extinguished only with life itself. But it is easy to see that, of all armies in the world, those in which advancement must be slowest in time of peace are the armies of democratic countries. As the number of commissions is naturally limited while the number of competitors is almost unlimited, and as the strict law of equality is over all alike, none can make rapid progress; many can make no progress at all. Thus

Ambitions of people in the military favor war

the desire of advancement is greater and the opportunities of advancement fewer there than elsewhere. All the ambitious spirits of a democratic army are consequently ardently desirous of war, because war makes vacancies and warrants the violation of that law of seniority which is the sole privilege natural to democracy.

2:281

Danger of an army in an unwarlike nation

62.   Moreover, as among democratic nations . . . to repeat what I have just remarked . . . the wealthiest, best-educated, and ablest men seldom adopt the military profession, the army, taken collectively, eventually forms a small nation by itself, where the mind is less enlarged and habits are more rude than in the nation at large. Now, this small uncivilized nation has arms in its possession and alone knows how to use them; for, indeed, the pacific temper of the community increases the danger to which a democratic people is exposed from the military and turbulent spirit of the army. Nothing is so dangerous as an army in the midst of an unwarlike nation; the excessive love of the whole community for quiet continually puts the constitution at the mercy of the soldiery.

2:282–83

Democracies and war

63.   There are two things that a democratic people will always find very difficult, to begin a war and to end it.

2:283

Wars threaten democracy

64.   All those who seek to destroy the liberties of a democratic nation ought to know that war is the surest and the shortest means to accomplish it. This is the first axiom of the science.

2:284

Effect of democratic upbringing on the military mind

65.   The remedy for the vices of the army is not to be found in the army itself, but in the country. Democratic nations are naturally afraid of disturbance and of despotism; the object is to turn these natural instincts into intelligent, deliberate, and lasting tastes. When men have at last learned to make a peaceful and profitable use of freedom and have felt its blessings, when they have conceived a manly love of order and have freely submit-

ted themselves to discipline, these same men, if they follow the profession of arms, bring into it, unconsciously and almost against their will, these same habits and manners. The general spirit of the nations, being infused into the spirit peculiar to the army, tempers the opinions and desires engendered by military life, or represses them by the mighty force of public opinion. Teach the citizens to be educated, orderly, firm, and free and the soldiers will be disciplined and obedient.

2:285

66. After all, and in spite of all precautions, a large army in the midst of a democratic people will always be a source of great danger. The most effectual means of diminishing that danger would be to reduce the army, but this is a remedy that all nations are not able to apply.

Only safe army in a democracy is a small one

2:285

67. If I am not mistaken, the least warlike and also the least revolutionary part of a democratic army will always be its chief commanders.

Commanders of democratic armies

2:288

68. I am therefore of the opinion that when a democratic people engages in a war after a long peace, it incurs much more risk of defeat than any other nation; but it ought not easily to be cast down by its reverses, for the chances of success for such an army are increased by the duration of the war. When a war has at length, by its long continuance, roused the whole community from their peaceful occupations and ruined their minor undertakings, the same passions that made them attach so much importance to the maintenance of peace will be turned to arms. War, after it has destroyed all modes of speculation, becomes itself the great and sole speculation, to which all the ardent and ambitious desires that equality engenders are exclusively directed. Hence it is that the selfsame democratic nations that are so reluctant to engage in hostilities sometimes perform prodigious achievements when once they have taken the field.

Performance of democratic armies usually excellent

2:292–93

Lure of military glory great in a democracy

69.   No kind of greatness is more pleasing to the imagination of a democratic people than military greatness, a greatness of vivid and sudden luster, obtained without toil, by nothing but the risk of life.

2:293

Effect of commerce and equality on war

70.   As the spread of equality, taking place in several countries at once, simultaneously impels their various inhabitants to follow manufactures and commerce, not only do their tastes become similar, but their interests are so mixed and entangled with one another that no nation can inflict evils on other nations without those evils falling back upon itself; and all nations ultimately regard war as a calamity almost as severe to the conqueror as to the conquered.

Thus, on the one hand, it is extremely difficult in democratic times to draw nations into hostilities; but, on the other, it is almost impossible that any two of them should go to war without embroiling the rest. The interests of all are so interlaced, their opinions and their wants so much alike, that none can remain quiet when the others stir. Wars therefore become more rare, but when they break out, they spread over a larger field.

2:297

Classic prediction of eventual U.S.–Russia confrontation

71.   There are at the present time two great nations in the world, which started from different points, but seem to tend towards the same end. I allude to the Russians and the Americans. Both of them have grown up unnoticed; and while the attention of mankind was directed elsewhere, they have suddenly placed themselves in the front rank among the nations, and the world learned their existence and their greatness at almost the same time.

All other nations seem to have nearly reached their natural limits, and they have only to maintain their power; but these are still in the act of growth. All the others have stopped, or continue to advance with extreme difficulty; these alone are proceeding with ease and celerity along a path to which no limit can be perceived. The American struggles against the obstacles that nature opposes to him; the adversaries of the Russian are men. The former combats the wilderness and savage life; the latter, civilization with all its arms. The conquests of the American are therefore gained by the plowshare; those of the Russian by the sword. The Anglo-American relies upon personal interest to accomplish his ends and gives free scope to the unguided strength and common sense of the people; the Russian centers all the authority of society in a single arm. The principal instrument of the former is freedom; of the latter, servitude. Their starting-point is different and their courses are not the same; yet each of them seems marked out by the will of heaven to sway the destinies of half the globe.

1:452

Revolution and Disunion: Can American democracy cope with them?

72. The circumstance which makes it easy to maintain a Federal government in America is not only that the states have similar interests, a common origin, and a common language, but that they have also arrived at the same stage of civilization, which almost always renders a union feasible. I do not know of any European nation, however small, that does not present less uniformity in its different provinces than the American people, which occupy a territory as extensive as one half of Europe.

Basis of strong federal government in America

1:176

73. [There are] three principal causes of the maintenance of the democratic republic—Federal union—Township institutions [and] —Judicial power.

Basis of American political unity

1:309

74. Single nations have therefore a natural tendency to centralization, and confederations to dismemberment.

Disintegrative tendency of federations

1:400

75. If, then, a state of society can ever be founded in which every man shall have something to keep and little to take from others, much will have been done for the peace of the world. . . .

Property stake in society discourages revolution

Between these two extremes of democratic communities [the poor and the wealthy] stands an innumerable multitude of men almost alike, who, without being exactly either rich or poor, possess sufficient property to desire the maintenance of order, yet not enough to excite envy. Such men are the natural enemies of violent commotions; their lack of agitation keeps all beneath them and above them still and secures the balance of the fabric of society.

2:266

Masses sense they, too, have stake in society

76. Hence in democratic communities the majority of the people do not clearly see what they have to gain by a revolution, but they continually and in a thousand ways feel that they might lose by one.

2:267

Effect of commerce on political stability

77. I know of nothing more opposite to revolutionary attitudes than commercial ones. Commerce is naturally adverse to all the violent passions; it loves to temporize, takes delight in compromise, and studiously avoids irritation. It is patient, insinuating, flexible, and never has recourse to extreme measures until obliged by the most absolute necessity. Commerce renders men independent of one another, gives them a lofty notion of their personal importance, leads them to seek to conduct their own affairs, and teaches how to conduct them well; it therefore prepares men for freedom, but preserves them from revolutions.

2:268

America—The most revolution-proof nation in the world

78. In no country in the world is the love of property more active and more anxious than in the United States; nowhere does the majority display less inclination for those principles which threaten to alter, in whatever manner, the laws of property.

2:270

Only real danger lies in inequality of conditions

79. If ever America undergoes great revolutions, they will be brought about by the presence of the black race on the soil of the United States; that is to say, they will

owe their origin, not to the equality, but to the inequality of condition.

2:270

80.   It must be described how, during revolutions, it is always a minority that rules. Always true of revolutions: it is only the spiritual state of the majority which makes this tyranny by a minority possible.

European Revolution, 108

Minority rules during revolution

81.   A new and terrible thing has come into the world, an immense new sort of revolution whose toughest agents are the least literate and most vulgar classes, while they are incited and their laws written by intellectuals.

European Revolution, 161

Revolutionaries are strange alliance of thugs and idealists

82.   True, we have seen issuing from the French Revolution a new kind of revolutionary, a turbulent and destructive type, always ready to demolish and unable to construct. He, however, is not merely violent; he scorns individual rights and persecutes minorities but, what is entirely new, he professes to justify all this. The idea that there are no individual rights but only a mass of people to whom everything is permitted is now elevated to a doctrine.

European Revolution, 162

Revolutionaries scorn civil liberties

83.   The pendular motion of our revolutions is illusory. It will not withstand close examination.

In the beginning always a movement toward decentralization: 1787, 1828, 1848. In the end a further extension of centralization.

In the beginning people follow some logic; in the end, they stumblingly follow their habits, their passions, power.

To sum up, the last word always rests with centralization, which grows deeper even when it seems less apparent on the surface, since the social movement, the atomization, and the isolation of social elements, always continues during such times.

European Revolution, 165

Revolutions always produce sharp increase in centralization

American Law and Lawyers: Their special importance to American
democracy

**Supreme
Court—The most
powerful judicial
body in the world**

84. When we have examined in detail the organization of the Supreme Court and the entire prerogatives
which it exercises, we shall readily admit that a more imposing judicial power was never constituted by any people. The Supreme Court is placed higher than any other
known tribunal, both by the nature of its rights and the
class of justiciable parties which it controls.

1:155

**Judicial power a
barrier to tyranny**

85. Within these limits the power vested in the American courts of justice of pronouncing a statute to be
unconstitutional forms one of the most powerful barriers
that have ever been devised against the tyranny of political assemblies.

1:107

**Lawyers are
security against
excesses of
democracy**

86. In visiting the Americans and studying their laws,
we perceive that the authority they have entrusted to
members of the legal profession, and the influence that
these individuals exercise in the government, are the
most powerful existing security against the excesses of
democracy.

1:283

**Legal profession is
closest American
approach to a
responsible
aristocratic class**

87. In America there are no nobles or literary men,
and the people are apt to mistrust the wealthy; lawyers
consequently form the highest political class and the
most cultivated portion of society. They have therefore
nothing to gain by innovation, which adds a conservative interest to their natural taste for public order. If I
were asked where I place the American aristocracy, I
should reply without hesitation that it is not among the
rich, who are united by no common tie, but that it occu-
pies the judicial bench and the bar.

The more we reflect upon all that occurs in the United
States, the more we shall be persuaded that the lawyers,
as a body, form the most powerful, if not the only, coun-
terpoise to the democratic element. In that country we
easily perceive how the legal profession is qualified by
its attributes, and even by its faults, to neutralize the

vices inherent in popular government. When the American people are intoxicated by passion or carried away
by the impetuosity of their ideas, they are checked and
stopped by the almost invisible influence of their legal
counselors. These secretly oppose their aristocratic propensities to the nation's democratic instincts, their su-
perstitious attachment to what is old to its love of novel-
ty, their narrow views to its immense designs, and their
habitual procrastination to its ardent impatience.

Armed with the power of declaring the laws to be
unconstitutional, the American magistrate perpetually
interferes in political affairs.

1:288–89

88.   The jury contributes powerfully to form the judgment and to increase the natural intelligence of a people; and this, in my opinion, is its greatest advantage. It
may be regarded as a gratuitous public school, ever
open, in which every juror learns his rights, enters into
daily communication with the most learned and enlightened members of the upper classes, and becomes practically acquainted with the laws, which are brought within the reach of his capacity by the efforts of the bar, the
advice of the judge, and even the passions of the parties. I think that the practical intelligence and political
good sense of the Americans are mainly attributable to
the long use that they have made of the jury in civil
causes.

I do not know whether the jury is useful to those who
have lawsuits, but I am certain it is highly beneficial to
those who judge them; and I look upon it as one of the
most efficacious means for the education of the people
which society can employ.

Jury system as a law school for the masses

1:295–96

Voluntary Associations: Are they the most efficient check to the tendency toward democratic despotism?

89.   The omnipotence of the majority appears to me to
be so full of peril to the American republics that the dangerous means used to bridle it seem to be more advan-
tageous than prejudicial. And here I will express an

Role of associations as a check against tyranny

opinion that may remind the reader of what I said when speaking of the freedom of townships. There are no countries in which associations are more needed to prevent the despotism of faction or the arbitrary power of a prince than those which are democratically constituted. In aristocratic nations the body of the nobles and the wealthy are in themselves natural associations which check the abuses of power. In countries where such associations do not exist, if private individuals cannot create an artificial and temporary substitute for them I can see no permanent protection against the most galling tyranny; and a great people may be oppressed with impunity by a small faction or by a single individual.

1:202

Voluntary associations require mature wisdom for effective citizen use

90.   It cannot be denied that the unrestrained liberty of association for political purposes is the privilege which a people is longest in learning how to exercise. If it does not throw the nation into anarchy, it perpetually augments the chances of that calamity. On one point, however, this perilous liberty offers a security against dangers of another kind; in countries where associations are free, secret societies are unknown. In America there are factions, but no conspiracies.

1:202–03

Is there an inalienable right of association?

91.   The most natural privilege of man, next to the right of acting for himself, is that of combining his exertions with those of his fellow creatures and of acting in common with them. The right of association therefore appears to me almost as inalienable in its nature as the right of personal liberty. No legislator can attack it without impairing the foundations of society. Nevertheless, if the liberty of association is only a source of advantage and prosperity to some nations, it may be perverted or carried to excess by others, and from an element of life may be changed into a cause of destruction.

1:203

How voluntary associations increase an individual's power

92.   Among democratic nations, on the contrary, all the citizens are independent and feeble; they can do hardly anything by themselves, and none of them can oblige his fellow men to lend him their assistance. They

all, therefore, become powerless if they do not learn voluntarily to help one another. If men living in democratic countries had no right and no inclination to associate for political purposes, their independence would be in great jeopardy, but they might long preserve their wealth and their cultivation: whereas if they never acquired the habit of forming associations in ordinary life, civilization itself would be endangered. A people among whom individuals lost the power of achieving great things singlehanded, without acquiring the means of producing them by united exertions, would soon relapse into barbarism.

2:115–16

93.   A government might perform the part of some of the largest American companies, and several states, members of the Union, have already attempted it; but what political power could ever carry on the vast multitude of lesser undertakings which the American citizens perform every day, with the assistance of the principle of association?. . . .

Danger if government displaces voluntary associations

The more it stands in the place of associations, the more will individuals, losing the notion of combining together, require its assistance. . . .

The morals and the intelligence of a democratic people would be as much endangered as its business and manufactures if the government ever wholly usurped the place of private companies.

2:116–17

94.   There is only one country on the face of the earth where the citizens enjoy unlimited freedom of association for political purposes. This same country is the only one in the world where the continual exercise of the right of association has been introduced into civil life and where all the advantages which civilization can confer are procured by means of it.

America unique in the world in its heavy use of voluntary associations

In all the countries where political associations are prohibited, civil associations are rare. It is hardly probable that this is the result of accident, but the inference should rather be that there is a natural and perhaps a necessary connection between these two kinds of associations.

2:123

Uses of voluntary associations

95. The power of the association has reached its highest degree in America. Associations are made for purposes of trade, and for political, literary and religious interests. It is never by recourse to a higher authority that one seeks success, but by an appeal to individual powers working in concert.

The last word in the way of an association seems to me to be the temperance societies, that is to say an association of men who mutually agree to abstain from a vice, and find in collective power an aid in resisting what is most intimate and personal to each man, his own inclinations. The effect of temperance societies is one of the most notable things in this country.

Journey to America, 212

One learns the power of associations only by experience

96. Now, it is solely in great associations that the general value of the principle of association is displayed. Citizens who are individually powerless do not very clearly anticipate the strength that they may acquire by uniting together; it must be shown to them in order to be understood.

2:124

A "dangerous freedom?"

97. Thus it is by the enjoyment of a dangerous freedom [associations] that the Americans learn the art of rendering the dangers of freedom less formidable.

2:127

Values of associations to a democracy

98. I firmly believe that an aristocracy cannot again be founded in the world, but I think that private citizens, by combining together, may constitute bodies of great wealth, influence, and strength, corresponding to the persons of an aristocracy. By this means many of the greatest political advantages of aristocracy would be obtained without its injustice or its dangers. An association for political, commercial, or manufacturing purposes, or even for those of science and literature, is a powerful and enlightened member of the community, which cannot be disposed of at pleasure or oppressed without remonstrance, and which, by defending its own rights against the encroachments of the government, saves the common liberties of the country.

2:342

3

American Social Structure and Democratic Egalitarian Beliefs

Although not a sociologist in the modern sense, Tocqueville is increasingly recognized today as a great pioneer of social science. He was deficient in sociological jargon, but superior in revealing the essence of social issues. His interest in the structure of society stemmed from sensitivity to *egalité,* which he applied especially to class, family, and race with almost terrifying clarity.

There is nothing antiquated about his conclusions: America had no aristocracy; all its society was melted into a single, fluid and open middle class; class existed here in a state of flux and relative instability. Family was dissolved by egalitarianism into individual atoms, held together tenuously by mutual happiness and bonds of affection. Race was the greatest problem of America, he concluded. No one has confronted this persistently intractable enigma more squarely or unsparingly than he.

A new Society: By intent? By ethnic differentiation?

1. In that land the great experiment of the attempt to construct society upon a new basis was to be made by civilized man; and it was there, for the first time, that theories hitherto unknown, or deemed impracticable, were to exhibit a spectacle for which the world had not been prepared by the history of the past.

Americans intended for their society to be new and different

1:26

2. America is the only country in which it has been possible to witness the natural and tranquil growth of society, and where the influence exercised on the future

America is the only current example of the

43

birth of a new society

condition of states by their origin is clearly distinguishable.

1:28

Common features united early Americans

3.   The emigrants who came at different periods to occupy the territory now covered by the American Union differed from each other in many respects; their aim was not the same, and they governed themselves on different principles.

These men had, however, certain features in common, and they were all placed in an analogous situation. The tie of language is, perhaps, the strongest and the most durable that can unite mankind. All the emigrants spoke the same language; they were all children of the same people.

1:29

Role of Irish and Catholic immigrants

4.   The greatest part of British America was peopled by men who, after having shaken off the authority of the Pope, acknowledged no other religious supremacy. . . .

About fifty years ago Ireland began to pour a Catholic population into the United States; and on their part, the Catholics of America made proselytes, so that, at the present moment more than a million Christians professing the truths of the Church of Rome are to be found in the Union. These Catholics are faithful to the observances of their religion; they are fervent and zealous in the belief of their doctrines. Yet they constitute the most republican and the most democratic class in the United States. This fact may surprise the observer at first, but the causes of it may easily be discovered upon reflection.

Catholic religion not necessarily hostile to democracy

I think that the Catholic religion has erroneously been regarded as the natural enemy of democracy. Among the various sects of Christians, Catholicism seems to me, on the contrary, to be one of the most favorable to equality of condition among men. In the Catholic Church the religious community is composed of only two elements: the priest and the people. The priest alone rises above the rank of his flock, and all below him are equal.

1:311

5.   If this tendency to assimilation brings foreign nations closer to each other, it must *a fortiori* prevent the
descendants of the same people from becoming aliens
to one another.

Importance of assimilation (The "Melting Pot") to a new and united society

The time will therefore come when one hundred and
fifty million men will be living in North America, equal in
condition, all belonging to one family, owing their origin
to the same cause, and preserving the same civilization,
the same language, the same religion, the same habits,
the same manners, and imbued with the same opinions,
propagated under the same forms. The rest is uncertain,
but this is certain; and it is a fact new to the world, a fact
that the imagination strives in vain to grasp.

Classic prediction on future of North America

1:451–52

Family Change: Creative or disintegrative?

6.   What is called family pride is often founded
upon an illusion of self-love. A man wishes to perpetu-
ate and immortalize himself, as it were, in his great-
grandchildren. Where family pride ceases to act, individual selfishness comes into play. When the idea of
family becomes vague, indeterminate, and uncertain, a
man thinks of his present convenience; he provides for
the establishment of his next succeeding generation and
no more.

Importance of family pride to constructive individual action

1:52

7.   In America the family, in the Roman and aristocratic signification of the word, does not exist. All that remains of it are a few vestiges in the first years of childhood, when the father exercises, without opposition,
that absolute domestic authority which the feebleness of
his children renders necessary and which their interest,
as well as his own incontestable superiority, warrants.
But as soon as the young American approaches manhood, the ties of filial obedience are relaxed day by day;
master of his thoughts, he is soon master of his conduct.
In America there is, strictly speaking, no adolescence: at
the close of boyhood the man appears and begins to
trace out his own path.

A different kind of family from the old world

2:202

Role of father changed

8. The father foresees the limits of his authority long beforehand, and when the time arrives, he surrenders it without a struggle; the son looks forward to the exact period at which he will be his own master, and he enters upon his freedom without precipitation and without effort, as a possession which is his own and which no one seeks to wrest from him.

2:203

Importance of new role of father for the permanence of democracy

9. Thus at the same time that the power of aristocracy is declining, the austere, the conventional, and the legal part of parental authority vanishes and a species of equality prevails around the domestic hearth. I do not know, on the whole, whether society loses by the change, but I am inclined to believe that man individually is a gainer by it. I think that in proportion as manners and laws become more democratic, the relation of father and son becomes more intimate and more affectionate; rules and authority are less talked of, confidence and tenderness are often increased, and it would seem that the natural bond is drawn closer in proportion as the social bond is loosened.

In a democratic family the father exercises no other power than that which is granted to the affection and the experience of age; his orders would perhaps be disobeyed, but his advice is for the most part authoritative. Though he is not hedged in with ceremonial respect, his sons at least accost him with confidence; they have no settled form of addressing him, but they speak to him constantly and are ready to consult him every day. The master and the constituted ruler have vanished; the father remains.

2:205–06

Brotherhood in the American family

10. In democratic countries, on the contrary, the language addressed by a son to his father is always marked by mingled freedom, familiarity, and affection, which at once show that new relations have sprung up in the bosom of the family.

A similar revolution takes place in the mutual relations of children. . . . Scarcely anything can occur to break the tie thus formed at the outset of life, for brotherhood brings them daily together without embarrassing them.

It is not, then, by interest, but by common associations and by the free sympathy of opinion and of taste that democracy unites brothers to each other. It divides their inheritance, but allows their hearts and minds to unite.

Such is the charm of these democratic manners that even the partisans of aristocracy are attracted by it. . . .

2:206–07

11. No free communities ever existed without morals, and . . . morals are the work of woman.

Role of women in the American family: girls

Among almost all Protestant nations young women are far more the mistresses of their own actions than they are in Catholic countries. . . .

In the United States the doctrines of Protestantism are combined with great political liberty and a most democratic state of society, and nowhere are young women surrendered so early or so completely to their own guidance.

Long before an American girl arrives at the marriageable age, her emanicipation from maternal control begins; she has scarcely ceased to be a child when she already thinks for herself, speaks with freedom, and acts on her own impulse. The great scene of the world is constantly open to her view; far from seeking to conceal it from her, it is every day disclosed more completely and she is taught to survey it with a firm and calm gaze.

2:209

12. It is rare that an American woman, at any age, displays childish timidity or ignorance. Like the young women of Europe she seeks to please, but she knows precisely the cost of pleasing. If she does not abandon herself to evil, at least she knows that it exists; and she is remarkable rather for purity of manners than for chastity of mind.

American girls different from those of Europe

2:209–10

13. Precocious marriages are rare. American women do not marry until their understandings are exercised and ripened, whereas in other countries most women generally begin to exercise and ripen their understandings only after marriage.

Role of women in America: wives

I by no means suppose, however, that the great change which takes place in all the habits of women in the United States as soon as they are married ought solely to be attributed to the constraint of public opinion; it is frequently imposed upon themselves by the sole effort of their own will. When the time for choosing a husband arrives, that cold and stern reasoning power which has been educated and invigorated by the free observation of the world teaches an American woman that a spirit of levity and independence in the bonds of marriage is a constant subject of annoyance, not of pleasure; it tells her that the amusements of the girl cannot become the recreations of the wife, and that the sources of a married woman's happiness are in the home of her husband. As she clearly discerns beforehand the only road that can lead to domestic happiness, she enters upon it at once and follows it to the end without seeking to turn back.

2:213

Danger of laxity of morals

14.   Society is endangered, not by the great profligacy of a few, but by laxity of morals among all. In the eyes of a legislator prostitution is less to be dreaded than intrigue.

2:219

Classic prediction of the future of women's rights in America

15.   I believe that [in America] the social changes that bring nearer to the same level the father and son, the master and servant, and, in general, superiors and inferiors will raise woman and make her more and more the equal of man.

2:222

European roots of modern radical feminism, as distinguished from evolutionary U.S. feminism

16.   There are people in Europe who, confounding together the different characteristics of the sexes, would make man and woman into beings not only equal but alike. They would give to both the same functions, impose on both the same duties, and grant to both the same rights; they would mix them in all things—their occupations, their pleasures, their business. It may readily be conceived that by thus attempting to make one sex equal to the other, both are degraded, and from so preposterous a medley of the works of nature nothing

could ever result but weak men and disorderly women.

It is not thus that the Americans understand that species of democratic equality which may be established between the sexes. They admit that as nature has appointed such wide differences between the physical and moral constitution of man and woman, her manifest design was to give a distinct employment to their various faculties; and they hold that improvement does not consist in making beings so dissimilar do pretty nearly the same things, but in causing each of them to fulfill their respective tasks in the best possible manner. The Americans have applied to the sexes the great principle of political economy which governs the manufacturers of our age, by carefully dividing the duties of man from those of woman in order that the great work of society may be the better carried on.

2:222–23

17. Nor have the Americans ever supposed that one consequence of democratic principles is the subversion of marital power or the confusion of the natural authorities in families. They hold that every association must have a head in order to accomplish its object, and that the natural head of the conjugal association is man. They do not therefore deny him the right of directing his partner, and they maintain that in the smaller association of husband and wife as well as in the great social community the object of democracy is to regulate and legalize the powers that are necessary, and not to subvert all power.

Women's authority in American family

This opinion is not peculiar to one sex and contested by the other; I never observed that the women of America consider conjugal authority as a[n un]fortunate usurpation of their rights, or that they thought themselves degraded by submitting to it. It appeared to me, on the contrary, that they attach a sort of pride to the voluntary surrender of their own will and make it their boast to bend themselves to the yoke, not to shake it off.

2:223

18. As for myself, I do not hesitate to avow that although the women of the United States are confined within the narrow circle of domestic life, and their situa-

Tocqueville's summation of women's status in America during 1830s

tion is in some respects one of extreme dependence, I have nowhere seen woman occupying a loftier position; and if I were asked, now that I am drawing to the close of this work, in which I have spoken of so many important things done by the Americans, to what the singular prosperity and growing strength of that people ought mainly to be attributed, I should reply; To the superiority of their women.

2:225

Social role of American and European women compared

19.   There is certainly no country in the world where the tie of marriage is more respected than in America or where conjugal happiness is more highly or worthily appreciated. . . .

While the European endeavors to forget his domestic troubles by agitating society, the American derives from his home that love of order which he afterwards carries with him into public affairs.

1:315

Morality, Customs, Leisure: Important, or merely quaint?

Importance of popular customs to American society

20.   The customs of the Americans of the United States are, then, the peculiar cause which renders that people the only one of the American nations that is able to support a democratic government; and it is the influence of customs that produces the different degrees of order and prosperity which may be distinguished in the several Anglo-American democracies. . . .

Too much importance is attributed to legislation, too little to customs. These three great causes serve, no doubt, to regulate and direct American democracy; but if they were to be classed in their proper order, I should say that physical circumstances are less efficient than the laws, and the laws infinitely less so than the customs of the people.

1:334

Social group tendencies in America

21.   The Americans, who mingle so readily in their political assemblies and courts of justice, are wont carefully to separate into small distinct circles in order to indulge by themselves in the enjoyments of private life. Each of

them willingly acknowledges all his fellow citizens as his equals, but will only receive a very limited number of them as his friends or his guests. This appears to me to be very natural. In proportion as the circle of public society is extended, it may be anticipated that the sphere of private intercourse will be contracted; far from supposing that the members of modern society will ultimately live in common, I am afraid they will end by forming only small coteries.

2:226–27

22. Nothing is more prejudicial to democracy than its outward forms of behavior; many men would willingly endure its vices who cannot support its manners. I cannot, however, admit that there is nothing commendable in the manners of a democratic people. . . . **Democratic manners (one type of customs)**

In democracies manners are never so refined as among aristocratic nations, but on the other hand they are never so coarse. Neither the coarse oaths of the populace nor the elegant and choice expressions of the nobility are to be heard there; the manners of such a people are often vulgar, but they are neither brutal nor mean.

I have already observed that in democracies no such thing as a regular code of good breeding can be laid down. . . . Thus it may be said, in one sense, that the effect of democracy is not exactly to give men any particular manners, but to prevent them from having manners at all.

2:230

23. When the inhabitant of a democracy is not urged by his wants, he is so at least by his desires; for of all the possessions that he sees around him, none are wholly beyond his reach. He therefore does everything in a hurry, he is always satisfied with "pretty well," and never pauses more than an instant to consider what he has been doing. His curiosity is at once insatiable and cheaply satisfied; for he cares more to know a great deal quickly than to know anything well; he has no time and but little taste to search things to the bottom. **Americans always in a hurry—the weakness of this habit**

Thus, then, a democratic people are grave because their social and political condition constantly leads them

to engage in serious occupations, and they act inconsid-
erably because they give but little time and attention to
each of these occupations. The habit of inattention must
be considered as the greatest defect of the democratic
character.

2:235

**American national
conceit and
individual "brag"**

24.   In democracies, as the conditions of life are very
fluctuating, men have almost always recently acquired
the advantages which they possess; the consequence is
that they feel extreme pleasure in exhibiting them, to
show others and convince themselves that they really
enjoy them. As at any instant these same advantages
may be lost, their possessors are constantly on the alert
and make a point of showing that they still retain them.
Men living in democracies love their country just as they
love themselves, and they transfer the habits of their private vanity to their vanity as a nation.

2:237

**How material
wealth affects
manners**

25.   The love of wealth is therefore to be traced, as either a principal or an accessory motive, at the bottom of
all that the Americans do; this gives to all their passions
a sort of family likeness and soon renders the survey of
them exceedingly wearisome. This perpetual recurrence
of the same passion is monotonous; the peculiar methods by which this passion seeks its own gratification are
not less so.

   In an orderly and peaceable democracy like the United States, where men cannot enrich themselves by war,
by public office, or by political confiscation, the love of
wealth mainly drives them into business and manufactures. Although these pursuits often bring about great
commotions and disasters, they cannot prosper without
strictly regular habits and a long routine of petty uniform
acts. The stronger the passion is, the more regular are
these habits and the more uniform are these acts. It may
be said that it is the vehemence of their desires that
makes the Americans so methodical; it perturbs their
minds, but it disciplines their lives.

2:240

26.   In America most of the rich men were formerly
poor; most of those who now enjoy leisure were ab-

sorbed in business during their youth; the consequence of this is that when they might have had a taste for study, they had no time for it, and when the time is at their disposal, they have no longer the inclination.

The taste for intellectual pleasures is lacking in America

There is no class, then, in America, in which the taste for intellectual pleasures is transmitted with hereditary fortune and leisure and by which the labors of the intellect are held in honor.

1:54

27. An American, instead of going in a leisure hour to dance merrily at some place of public resort as the fellows of his class continue to do throughout the greater part of Europe, shuts himself up at home to drink. He thus enjoys two pleasures; he can go on thinking of his business and can get drunk decently by his own fireside.

Americans use of leisure time: Getting drunk

2:232

Class: Why Marxists don't like Tocqueville

28. The Americans never use the word *peasant*, because they have no idea of the class which that term denotes; the ignorance of more remote ages, the simplicity of rural life, and the rusticity of the villager have not been preserved among them. . . .

Absence of "peasant" concept from American life

1:328

29. Men living in this state of society cannot derive their belief from the opinions of the class to which they belong; for, so to speak, there are no longer any classes, or those which still exist are composed of such mobile elements that the body can never exercise any real control over its members.

America—a classless society

2:4

30. Nothing is more wretchedly corrupt than aristocracy which retains its wealth when it has lost its power and which still enjoys a vast amount of leisure after it is reduced to mere vulgar pastimes. The energetic passions and great conceptions that animated it heretofore leave it then, and nothing remains to it but a host of petty

America lacks the problem of a dying aristocratic class

consuming vices, which cling about it like worms upon a
carcass.

2:220

**The middle-class
character of our
classless society**

31. Up to now it seems to me that this country illus-
trates the most complete external development of the
middle classes, or rather that the whole of society seems
to have turned into one middle class. No one seems to
have the elegant manners and refined politeness of the
upper classes in Europe. On the contrary one is at once
struck by something vulgar, and a disagreeable casual-
ness of behaviour. But also no one has what we should
call *mauvais ton* in France. All the Americans that we
have yet met, right down to the simple shop-assistant,
seem to have had, or to wish to appear to have had, a
good education. Their manners are sober, poised and
reserved, and they all wear the same clothes.

Journey to America, 274

Reform: Compared to revolution, as a device for change

**Democracy versus
the police state in
crime control**

32. In America the means that the authorities have at
their disposal for the discovery of crimes and the arrest
of criminals are few. A state police does not exist, and
passports are unknown. The criminal police of the United States cannot be compared with that of France; the
magistrates and public agents are not numerous; they
do not always initiate the measures for arresting the
guilty; and the examinations of prisoners are rapid and
oral. Yet I believe that in no country does crime more
rarely elude punishment. The reason is that everyone

**Cooperative
voluntary
associations as the
mass base of
crime control**

conceives himself to be interested in furnishing evidence
of the crime and in seizing the delinquent. During my
stay in the United States I witnessed the spontaneous
formation of committees in a county for the pursuit and
prosecution of a man who had commited a great crime.
In Europe a criminal is an unhappy man who is strug-
gling for his life against the agents of power, while the
people are merely a spectator of the conflict; in America
he is looked upon as an enemy of the human race, and
the whole of mankind is against him.

1:99

33.   Someone observed to me one day in Philadelphia **Cheap liquor and** that almost all crimes in America are caused by the **crime** abuse of intoxicating liquors, which the lower classes can procure in great abundance because of their cheapness.

1:239

34.   The more equal social conditions become, the **Equality as a basic** more do men display this reciprocal disposition to oblige **source of the** each other. In democracies no great benefits are con- **philanthropic** ferred, but good offices are constantly rendered; a man **spirit** seldom displays self-devotion, but all men are ready to be of service to one another.

2:186

35.   ... The general extension of wealth and educa- **The trend from** tion which has made individuals more and more alike **private charity to** have given an immense and unexpected impetus to the **public duty** principle of equality, which Christianity had established in the spiritual rather than in the tangible material sphere. The idea that *all* men have a right to certain goods, to certain pleasures and that our primary moral duty is to procure these for them—this idea, as I said above, has now gained immense breadth, and it now appears in an endless variety of aspects. This first innovation led to another. Christianity made charity a personal virtue. Every day now we are making a social duty, a political obligation, a public virtue, out of it. And the growing number of those who must be supported, the variety of needs which we are growing accustomed to provide for, the disappearance of great personalities to whom previously one could turn with these problems of succor, now makes every eye turn to the State.

Correspondence with Gobineau, 193

Race: America's greatest future problem

36.   The human beings who are scattered over this **Three races** space do not form, as in Europe, so many branches of **plentiful in** the same stock. Three races, naturally distinct, and, I **America, unlike** might almost say, hostile to each other, are discoverable **Europe** among them at the first glance. Almost insurmountable

barriers had been raised between them by education
and law, as well as by their origin and outward characteristics; but fortune has brought them together on the
same soil, where, although they are mixed, they do not
amalgamate, and each race fulfills its destiny apart.

1:344

Racial limits to
the American
melting pot.

37.   The lot of the Negro is placed on the extreme limit
of servitude, while that of the Indian lies on the utter-
most verge of liberty; and slavery does not produce
more fatal effects upon the first than independence
upon the second. . . .

The Negro, who earnestly desires to mingle his race
with that of the European, cannot do so; while the Indian, who might succeed to a certain extent, disdains to
make the attempt. The servility of the one dooms him to
slavery, the pride of the other to death.

1:346–47

The melding of
blacks and whites
unlikely

38.   When I remember the extreme difficulty with
which aristocratic bodies, of whatever nature they may
be, are commingled with the mass of the people, and
the exceeding care which they take to preserve for ages
the ideal boundaries of their caste inviolate, I despair of
seeing an aristocracy disappear which is founded upon
visible and indelible signs. Those who hope that the Europeans will ever be amalgamated with the Negroes appear to me to delude themselves. I am not led to any
such conclusion by my reason or by the evidence of
facts. Hitherto wherever the whites have been the most
powerful, they have held the blacks in degradation or in
slavery; wherever the Negroes have been strongest,
they have destroyed the whites: this has been the only
balance that has ever taken place between the two
races.

1:373

Population and
assimilation
prospects for
American blacks

39.   . . . The white population grows by its natural increase, and at the same time by the immense influx of
immigrants; while the black population receives no immigrants and is upon its decline. The proportion that existed between the two races is soon inverted. The Negroes constitute a scanty remnant, a poor tribe of

vagrants, lost in the midst of an immense people who own the land; and the presence of the blacks is only marked by the injustice and the hardships of which they are the victims.

1:383

40. As soon as it is admitted that the whites and the emancipated blacks are placed upon the same territory in the situation of two foreign communities, it will readily be understood that there are but two chances for the future: the Negroes and the whites must either wholly part or wholly mingle. I have already expressed my conviction as to the latter event. I do not believe that the white and black races will ever live in any country upon an equal footing. But I believe the difficulty to be still greater in the United States than elsewhere. An isolated individual may surmount the prejudices of religion, of his country, or of his race; and if this individual is a king, he may effect surprising changes in society; but a whole people cannot rise, as it were, above itself. A despot who should subject the Americans and their former slaves to the same yoke might perhaps succeed in commingling their races; but as long as the American democracy remains at the head of affairs, no one will undertake so difficult a task; and it may be foreseen that the freer the white population of the United States becomes, the more isolated will it remain.

Future of race relations and assimilation

I have previously observed that the mixed race is the true bond of union between the Europeans and the Indians; just so, the mulattoes are the true means of transition between the white and the Negro; so that wherever mulattoes abound, the intermixture of the two races is not impossible. In some parts of America the European and the Negro races are so crossed with one another that it is rare to meet with a man who is entirely black or entirely white; when they have arrived at this point, the two races may really be said to be combined, or, rather, to have been absorbed in a third race, which is connected with both without being identical with either.

Effect of mixed races

Of all Europeans, the English are those who have mixed least with the Negroes. More mulattoes are to be seen in the South of the Union than in the North, but infinitely fewer than in any other European colony.

1:388–89

Predictions on the course of race relations

41. If I were called upon to predict the future, I should say that the abolition of slavery in the South will, in the common course of things, increase the repugnance of the white population for the blacks. I base this opinion upon the analogous observations I have already made in the North. I have remarked that the white inhabitants of the North avoid the Negroes with increasing care in proportion as the legal barriers of separation are removed by the legislature; and why should not the same result take place in the South? In the North the whites are deterred from intermingling with the blacks by an imaginary danger; in the South, where the danger would be real, I cannot believe that the fear would be less.

If, on the one hand, it be admitted (and the fact is unquestionable) that the colored population perpetually accumulate in the extreme South and increase more rapidly than the whites; and if, on the other hand, it be allowed that it is impossible to foresee a time at which the whites and the blacks will be so intermingled as to derive the same benefits from society, must it not be inferred that the blacks and the whites will, sooner or later, come to open strife in the Southern states? But if it be asked what the issue of the struggle is likely to be, it will readily be understood that we are here left to vague conjectures. The human mind may succeed in tracing a wide circle, as it were, which includes the future; but within that circle chance rules, and eludes all our foresight. In every picture of the future there is a dim spot which the eye of the understanding cannot penetrate. It appears, however, extremely probable that in the West Indies islands the white race is destined to be subdued, and upon the continent the blacks.

1:390–91

What race war would mean to America

42. Yet, at whatever period the strife may break out, the whites of the South, even if they are abandoned to their own resources, will enter the lists with an immense superiority of knowledge and the means of warfare; but the blacks will have numerical strength and the energy of despair upon their side, and these are powerful resources to men who have taken up arms. The fate of the white population of the Southern states will perhaps be

similar to that of the Moors in Spain. After having occupied the land for centuries, it will perhaps retire by degrees to the country whence its ancestors came and abandon to the Negroes the possession of a territory which Providence seems to have destined for them, since they can subsist and labor in it more easily than the whites.

The danger of a conflict between the white and the black inhabitants of the Southern states of the Union (a danger which, however remote it may be, is inevitable) perpetually haunts the imagination of the Americans, like a painful dream. The inhabitants of the North make it a common topic of conversation, although directly they have nothing to fear from it; but they vainly endeavor to devise some means of obviating the misfortunes which they foresee. In the Southern states the subject is not discusssed: the planter does not allude to the future in conversing with strangers; he does not communicate his apprehensions to his friends; he seeks to conceal them from himself. But there is something more alarming in the tacit forebodings of the South than in the clamorous fears of the North.

Differing attitudes, North and South

1:391–92

43. I am obliged to confess that I do not regard the abolition of slavery as a means of warding off the struggle of the two races in the Southern states. The Negroes may long remain slaves without complaining; but if they are once raised to the level of freemen, they will soon revolt at being deprived of almost all their civil rights; and as they cannot become the equals of the whites, they will speedily show themselves as enemies.

Prediction of rise of civil rights movement

1:394

44. I admit that I could not believe how you could fail to see the difficulty of reconciling your scientific theories with the letter and with the spirit of Christianity. About the letter: what is clearer in Genesis than the unity of the human race and the descent of all men from the same ancestor? About the spirit: is it not its unique trait to have abolished those racial distinctions which the Jewish religion still retained and to have made therefrom but one human race, all of whose members are equally

Tocqueville's denunciation of racism, as expressed by Gobineau

capable of improving and uniting themselves? How can this spirit—and I am trying to use plain common sense —be reconciled with a doctrine that makes races distinct and unequal, with differing capacities of understanding, of judgement, of action, due to some original and immutable disposition which invisibly denies the possibility of improvement for certain peoples? Evidently Christianity wishes to make all men brothers and equals. Your doctrine makes them cousins at best whose common father is very far away in the heavens; to you down here there are only victors and vanquished, masters and slaves, due to their different birthrights. This is obvious, since your doctrines are being approved, cited, commented upon by whom? by slaveowners and by those who favor the perpetuation of slavery on the basis of radical differences of race. I well know that right now there are in the south of the United States Christian pastors and perhaps even good priests (though they are slaveowners) who preach from their pulpit doctrines which are undoubtedly analogous with yours. But be assured that the majority of Christians, consisting of those whose interests do not subconsciously incline them toward your ideas—be assured, I say, that the majority of Christians of this world cannot have the least sympathy for your doctrines.

Special reference to America

Correspondence with Gobineau, 305–06.

4

Early Democratic National Culture:
Nature and Prospects

Tocqueville was quite curious to discover what kind of a high culture American democracy had produced. He soon found himself forced to concede that the new nation's culture was primitive—hardly more than a cultural colony of England, as the European conservatives had always believed to be the case. Unlike the Tories, however, Tocqueville did not attribute this to democratic government. He blamed the cultural situation not upon democracy, but upon the leveling, egalitarian spirit.

Three aspects of American culture drew most of his attention. Religion he considered a dynamic force, helpful to future cultural development, friendly to democracy and important for democracy to protect. Tocqueville liked its sincerity, and the separation of church and state he admired for its invigorating effect and its apparent tendency to make religion a democratic force. Religion in America showed how the principle of self-interest, rightly understood, could promote a moral and healthy society.

Education was the second aspect, but here the young Frenchman was tentative. He certainly endorsed public education in a democracy as a means of correcting misinformation and informing the young of their democratic rights and duties. On the other hand, he felt that the public schools taught a consensus on hazy generalities, and avoided controversial problems. However, this cautiousness about American education may have resulted in part from his personal lack of public school experience. He noted the few libraries and sparse holdings of books which made impossible an education advanced in depth, and he regretted the absence of quality newspapers. Certainly he endorsed the need for continued educational progress.

61

As for the arts, here he was least enthusiastic, and found almost nothing worth preserving. However, he did offer hope for a better future, while deploring the present shoddy imitations, the appeal to passions instead of taste, and the absence of a national cultural style. What passed for culture in America was designed for leisure diversions, not a guide to active life, and consequently American culture was flat and tasteless.

The same criticisms are still being made today, which gives Tocqueville's suggestions for improvement a special interest.

Religion and its Function in a Democratic Society

"Republican religion"
1. The greatest part of British America was peopled by men who, after having shaken off the authority of the Pope, acknowledged no other religious supremacy: they brought with them into the New World a form of Christianity which I cannot better describe than by styling it a democratic and republican religion. This contributed powerfully to the establishment of a republic and a democracy in public affairs; and from the beginning, politics and religion contracted an alliance which has never been dissolved.

1:311

Religion, a guide to public behavior
2. Thus, while the law permits the Americans to do what they please, religion prevents them from conceiving, and forbids them to commit, what is rash or unjust.
Religion in America takes no direct part in the government of society, but it must be regarded as the first of their political institutions; for if it does not impart a taste for freedom, it facilitates the use of it.

1:316

Separation of church and state in America makes religion democratic
3. On my arrival in the United States the religious aspect of the country was the first thing that struck my attention; and the longer I stayed there, the more I perceived the great political consequences resulting from this new state of things. In France I had almost always seen the spirit of religion and the spirit of freedom

marching in opposite directions. But in America I found they were intimately united and that they reigned in common over the same country. My desire to discover the causes of this phenomenon increased from day to day. In order to satisfy it I questioned the members of all the different sects; I sought especially the society of the clergy, who are the depositaries of the different creeds and are especially interested in their duration. As a member of the Roman Catholic Church, I was more particularly brought into contact with several of its priests, with whom I became intimately acquainted. To each of these men I expressed my astonishment and explained my doubts. I found that they differed upon matters of detail alone, and that they all attributed the peaceful dominion of religion in their country mainly to the separation of church and state. I do not hesitate to affirm that during my stay in America I did not meet a single individual, of the clergy or the laity, who was not of the same opinion on this point.

1:319–20

4. Perhaps, however, this great utility of religions is still more obvious among nations where equality of conditions prevails than among others. It must be acknowledged that equality, which brings great benefits into the world, nevertheless suggests to men (as will be shown hereafter) some very dangerous propensities. It tends to isolate them from one another, to concentrate every man's attention upon himself; and it lays open the soul to an inordinate love of material gratification. . . .

Special utility of religion in a republic

There is no religion that does not place the object of man's desires above and beyond the treasures of earth and that does not naturally raise his soul to regions far above those of the senses. Nor is there any which does not impose on man some duties towards his kind and thus draw him at times from the contemplation of himself. . . .

Religious nations are therefore naturally strong on the very point on which democratic nations are weak; this shows of what importance it is for men to preserve their religion as their conditions become more equal.

2:23

**Religion a
corrective to
materialism**

5. The taste for well-being is the prominent and indelible feature of democratic times. . . .

The chief concern of religion is to purify, to regulate,
and to restrain the excessive and exclusive taste for well-
being that men feel in periods of equality; but it would
be an error to attempt to overcome it completely or to
eradicate it. Men cannot be cured of the love of riches,
but they may be persuaded to enrich themselves by
none but honest means.

2:27

**Basis of morality
in a democratic
society**

6. The Americans show by their practice that they
feel the high necessity of imparting morality to democratic communities by means of religion. What they
think of themselves in this respect is a truth of which every democratic nation ought to be thoroughly persuaded.

2:152–53

**Religion a
restraint on
materialism**

7. Materialism, among all nations, is a dangerous disease of the human mind; but it is more especially to be
dreaded among a democratic people because it readily
amalgamates with that vice which is most familiar to the
heart under such circumstances. Democracy encourages a taste for physical gratification; this taste, if it become excessive, soon disposes men to believe that all is
matter only; and materialism, in its turn, hurries them on
with mad impatience to these same delights; such is the
fatal circle within which democratic nations are driven
round. It were well that they should see the danger and
hold back.

Most religions are only general, simple, and practical
means of teaching men the doctrine of the immortality
of the soul. That is the greatest benefit which a democratic people derives from its belief, and hence belief is
more necessary to such a people than to all others.
When, therefore, any religion has struck its roots deep
into a democracy, beware that you do not disturb it; but
rather watch it carefully, as the most precious bequest of
aristocratic ages. Do not seek to supersede the old religious opinions of men by new ones, lest in the passage
from one faith to another, the soul being left for a while

stripped of all belief, the love of physical gratifications should grow upon it and fill it wholly.

2:154–55

8. I am so much alive to the almost inevitable dangers which beset religious belief whenever the clergy take part in public affairs, and I am so convinced that Christianity must be maintained at any cost in the bosom of modern democracies, that I had rather shut up the priesthood within the sanctuary than allow them to step beyond it.

2:156

Clergy should not enter politics

9. I believe that the sole effectual means which governments can employ in order to have the doctrine of the immortality of the soul duly respected is always to act as if they believed in it themselves; and I think that it is only by scrupulous conformity to religious morality in great affairs that they can hope to teach the community at large to know, to love, and to observe it in the lesser concerns of life.

2:156

Government should aid religion only by example

10. If men were ever to content themselves with material objects, it is probable that they would lose by degrees the art of producing them; and they would enjoy them in the end, like the brutes, without discernment and without improvement.

2:157

Dangers of materialism

11. When men have once allowed themselves to think no more of what is to befall them after life, they readily lapse into that complete and brutal indifference to futurity which is but too conformable to some propensities of mankind. As soon as they have lost the habit of placing their chief hopes upon remote events, they naturally seek to gratify without delay their smallest desires; and no sooner do they despair of living forever, than they are disposed to act as if they were to exist but for a single day.

2:158–59

Materialism promotes disregard of the future

12. He [the leader] must constantly endeavor to show his contemporaries that even in the midst of the perpet-

Democratic leadership must fight these materialist tendencies

ual commotion around them it is easier than they think to conceive and to execute protracted undertakings. He must teach them that although the aspect of mankind may have changed, the methods by which men may provide for their prosperity in this world are still the same; and that among democratic nations as well as elsewhere it is only by resisting a thousand petty selfish passions of the hour that the general and unquenchable passion for happiness can be satisfied. . . .

At all times it is important that those who govern nations should act with a view to the future: but this is even more necessary in democratic and skeptical ages than in any others.

2:159

Society not anti-Christian, really

13.   Our society is much more alienated from the theology than it is from the philosophy of Christianity.
Correspondence with Gobineau, 192

Christianity first introduced the idea of human brotherhood

14.   Christianity and consequently its morality went beyond all political powers and nationalities. Its grand achievement is to have formed a human community beyond national societies.
Correspondence with Gobineau, 192

Modern morality still based on Christianity

15.   Among these really new apparitions (and I think there may be a few attractive ones among them) the majority seem to derive directly from Christianity. They are only the applications of Christianity to a larger sphere, to other political forms, and to a very different social state. They are, briefly, the new consequences of an old principle.
Correspondence with Gobineau, 207–08

Importance of religion to American democracy

16.   I think that the state of religion in America is one of the things that most powerfully helps us to maintain our republican institutions. The religious spirit exercises a direct power over political passions, and also an indirect power by sustaining morals. It is because many enlightened Americans are convinced of this truth that not only do they not show the doubts they may have about the reality of Christianity, but even hesitate to join new sects such as the Unitarians. They are afraid that they may

lead indirectly to the destruction of the Christian religion, which would be an irreparable ill for humanity.

Journey to America, 114

Informal and Formal Education

17. In countries where the doctrine of the sovereignty of the people ostensibly prevails, the censorship of the press is not only dangerous, but absurd.

1:190

Press censorship absurd

18. In America political life is active, varied, even agitated, but is rarely affected by those deep passions which are excited only when material interests are impaired; and in the United States these interests are prosperous. A glance at a French and an American newspaper is sufficient to show the difference that exists in this respect between the two nations. In France the space allotted to commercial advertisements is very limited, and the news intelligence is not considerable, but the essential part of the journal is the discussion of the politics of the day. In America three-quarters of the enormous sheet are filled with advertisements, and the remainder is frequently occupied by political intelligence or trivial anecdotes; it is only from time to time that one finds a corner devoted to passionate discussions like those which the journalists of France every day give to their readers.

1:192

How American press differs from the French

19. It has been demonstrated by observation, and discovered by the sure instinct even of the pettiest despots, that the influence of a power is increased in proportion as its direction is centralized. In France the press combines a twofold centralization; almost all its power is centered in the same spot and, so to speak, in the same hands, for its organs are far from numerous. The influence upon a skeptical nation of a public press thus constituted must be almost unbounded. It is an enemy with whom a government may sign an occasional truce, but which it is difficult to resist for any length of time.

Role of centralization in freedom of press

Neither of these kinds of centralization exists in America. The United States has no metropolis; the intelligence and the power of the people are disseminated through all the parts of this vast country, and instead of radiating from a common point they cross each other in every direction; the Americans have nowhere established any central direction of opinion, any more than of the conduct of affairs. . . .

. . . the number of periodical and semi-periodical publications in the United States is almost incredibly large. The most enlightened Americans attribute the little influence of the press to this excessive dissemination of its power; and it is an axiom of political science in that country that the only way to neutralize the effect of the public journals is to multiply their number. I cannot see how a truth which is so self-evident should not already have been more generally admitted in Europe. I can see why the persons who hope to bring about revolutions by means of the press should be desirous of confining it to a few powerful organs, but it is inconceivable that the official partisans of the existing state of things and the natural supporters of the laws should attempt to diminish the influence of the press by concentrating its power.

1:192–93

How journalists differ in the two countries

20.   The class spirit of the French journalists consists in a violent but frequently an eloquent and lofty manner of discussing the great interests of the state, and the exceptions to this mode of writing are only occasional. The characteristics of the American journalist consist in an open and coarse appeal to the passions of his readers; he abandons principles to assail the characters of individuals, to track them into private life and disclose all their weaknesses and vices.

1:194

Extent of American press influence

21.   But although the press is limited to these resources, its influence in America is immense. It causes political life to circulate through all the parts of that vast territory. Its eye is constantly open to detect the secret springs of political designs and to summon the leaders of all parties in turn to the bar of public opinion. . . .

In the United States each separate journal exercises but little authority; but the power of the periodical press is secondary only to that of the people.

1:195

22. The more I consider the independence of the press in its principal consequences, the more am I convinced that in the modern world it is the chief and, so to speak, the constitutive element of liberty. A nation that is determined to remain free is therefore right in demanding, at any price, the exercise of this independence.

Importance of free press to America

1:200

23. When men are no longer united among themselves by firm and lasting ties, it is impossible to obtain the co-operation of any great number of them unless you can persuade every man whose help you require that his private interest obliges him voluntarily to unite his exertions to the exertions of all the others. This can be habitually and conveniently effected only by means of a newspaper; nothing but a newspaper can drop the same thought into a thousand minds at the same moment. A newspaper is an adviser that does not require to be sought, but that comes of its own accord and talks to you briefly every day of the common weal, without distracting you from your private affairs.

The value of the press to society

Newspapers therefore become more necessary in proportion as men become more equal and individualism more to be feared. To suppose that they only serve to protect freedom would be to diminish their importance: they maintain civilization. I shall not deny that in democratic countries newspapers frequently lead the citizens to launch together into very ill-digested schemes; but if there were no newspapers there would be no common activity. The evil which they produce is therefore much less than that which they cure.

2:119

24. ... the number of newspapers must diminish or increase among a democratic people in proportion as its administration is more or less centralized. ...

Why number of papers is large or small

The extraordinary subdivision of administrative power has much more to do with the enormous number of
American newspapers than the great political freedom
of the country and the absolute liberty of the press.

2:120–21

**Importance of
having many
papers**

25.   I am of the opinion that a democratic people without any national representative assemblies but with a
great number of small local powers would have in the
end more newspapers than another people governed
by a centralized administration and an elective legislature. What best explains to me the enormous circulation
of the daily press in the United States is that among the
Americans I find the utmost national freedom combined
with local freedom of every kind. . . .

Newspapers increase in numbers, not according to
their cheapness, but according to the more or less frequent want which a great number of men may feel for
intercommunication and combination.

2:121

**Egalitarian effect
of the press**

26.   A newspaper can survive only on the condition of
publishing sentiments or principles common to a large
number of men. . . .

The power of the newspaper press must therefore increase as the social conditions of men become more
equal.

2:122

**American distaste
for theory**

27.   The spirit of the Americans is averse to general
ideas; it does not seek theoretical discoveries.

1:326

**Effectiveness of
public education**

28.   The observer who is desirous of forming an
opinion on the state of instruction among the Anglo-
Americans must consider the same object from two different points of view. If he singles out only the learned,
he will be astonished to find how few they are; but if he
counts the ignorant, the American people will appear to
be the most enlightened in the world. The whole population, as I observed in another place, is situated between these two extremes.

1:326–27

29. It cannot be doubted that in the United States the instruction of the people powerfully contributes to the support of the democratic republic; and such must always be the case, I believe, where the instruction which enlightens the understanding is not separated from the moral education which amends the heart. But I would not exaggerate this advantage, and I am still further from thinking, as so many people do think in Europe, that men can be instantaneously made citizens by teaching them to read and write. True information is mainly derived from experience; and if the Americans had not been gradually accustomed to govern themselves, their book-learning would not help them much at the present day.

American education complements experience

1:329

30. But if you question him respecting his own country, the cloud that dimmed his intelligence will immediately disperse; his language will become as clear and precise as his thoughts. He will inform you what his rights are and by what means he exercises them; he will be able to point out the customs which obtain in the political world. You will find that he is well acquainted with the rules of the administration, and that he is familiar with the mechanism of the laws. The citizen of the United States does not acquire his practical science and his positive notions from books; the instruction he has acquired may have prepared him for receiving those ideas, but it did not furnish them. The American learns to know the laws by participating in the act of legislation; and he takes a lesson in the forms of government from governing. The great work of society is ever going on before his eyes and, as it were, under his hands.

An education favorably disposed toward experience makes for good citizens

1:329–30

31. Almost all the inhabitants of the territory of the Union are the descendants of a common stock; they speak the same language, they worship God in the same manner, they are affected by the same physical causes and they obey the same laws. Whence, then, do their characteristic differences arise? Why, in the Eastern

American education, unlike Europe, is citizenship-oriented

states of the Union, does the republican government display vigor and regularity and proceed with mature deliberation? Whence does it derive the wisdom and the durability which mark its acts, while in the Western states, on the contrary, society seems to be ruled by chance? There public business is conducted with an irregularity and a passionate, almost feverish excitement which do not announce a long or sure duration.

I am no longer comparing the Anglo-Americans with foreign nations; I am contrasting them with each other and endeavoring to discover why they are so unlike. The arguments that are derived from the nature of the country and the difference of legislation are here all set aside. Recourse must be had to some other cause; and what other cause can there be, except the customs of the people?

1:333

Classics as a deterrent to cheapening of democracy, for leadership education

32.   It is evident that in democratic communities the interest of individuals as well as the security of the commonwealth demands that the education of the greater number should be scientific, commercial, and industrial rather than literary. Greek and Latin should not be taught in all the schools; but it is important that those who, by their natural dispositions or their fortune, are destined to cultivate letters or prepared to relish them should find schools where a complete knowledge of ancient literature may be acquired and where the true scholar may be formed. A few excellent universities would do more towards the attainment of this object than a multitude of bad grammar-schools, where superfluous matters, badly learned, stand in the way of sound instruction in necessary studies.

All who aspire to literary excellence in democratic nations ought frequently to refresh themselves at the springs of ancient literature; there is no more wholesome medicine for the mind. Not that I hold the literary productions of the ancients to be irreproachable, but I think that they have some special merits, admirably calculated to counterbalance our peculiar defects. They are a prop on the side on which we are most in danger of falling.

2:66–67

33. Give democratic nations education and freedom and leave them alone. They will soon learn to draw from this world all the benefits that it can afford; they will improve each of the useful arts and will day by day render life more comfortable, more convenient, and more easy.

Importance of education to a democracy

2:153

34. From this new perception of the occupations of the lower classes results a principle, not entirely unknown to Christianity but one to which our times are giving a much broader and greater application: the right of the poor to education. The necessity to enlighten the masses is today hardly contested at all. And not only the basic principles of religion are to be taught them, but they are to be introduced to scientific and literary progress as far as possible; in brief, they are called forth to share all the fruits of the human intellect.

Right of the poor to an education

Correspondence with Gobineau, 200–01.

The Arts Under American Democracy

35. It must be acknowledged that in few of the civilized nations of our time have the higher sciences made less progress than in the United States; and in few have great artists, distinguished poets, or celebrated writers been more rare. Many Europeans, struck by this fact, have looked upon it as a natural and inevitable result of equality; and they have thought that if a democratic state of society and democratic institutions were ever to prevail over the whole earth, the human mind would gradually find its beacon lights grow dim, and men would relapse into a period of darkness.

Americans, despite poor record, have a taste for culture

I am convinced, however, that if the Americans had been alone in the world, with the freedom and the knowledge acquired by their forefathers and the passions which are their own, they would not have been slow to discover that progress cannot long be made in the application of the sciences without cultivating the theory of them; that all the arts are perfected by one another: and, however absorbed they might have been by the pursuit of the principal object of their desires, they would speedily have admitted that it is necessary to turn aside from it occasionally in order the better to attain it in the end.

2:36–37

Americans best in applied arts, not theory

36.   In America the purely practical part of science is admirably understood, and careful attention is paid to the theoretical portion which is immediately requisite to application. On this head the Americans always display a clear, free, original, and inventive power of mind. But hardly anyone in the United States devotes himself to the essentially theoretical and abstract portion of human knowledge. In this respect the Americans carry to excess a tendency that is, I think, discernible, though in a less degree, among all democratic nations.

2:43

American "hurry"

37.   Men who live in democratic communities not only seldom indulge in meditation, but they naturally entertain very little esteem for it.

2:44

American strengths in scientific culture

38.   I believe, moreover, in high scientific vocations. If the democratic principle does not, on the one hand, induce men to cultivate science for its own sake, on the other it enormously increases the number of those who do cultivate it. Nor is it credible that among so great a multitude a speculative genius should not from time to time arise inflamed by the love of truth alone. . . .

. . . permanent inequality of conditions leads men to confine themselves to the arrogant and sterile research for abstract truths, while the social condition and the institutions of democracy prepare them to seek the immediate and useful practical results of the sciences. This tendency is natural and inevitable; it is curious to be acquainted with it, and it may be necessary to point it out.

2:47

Effects of democracy upon artistic activity

39.   It commonly happens that in the ages of privilege the practice of almost all the arts becomes a privilege, and that every profession is a separate sphere of action, into which it is not allowable for everyone to enter. Even when productive industry is free, the fixed character that

belongs to aristocratic nations gradually segregates all the persons who practice the same art till they form a distinct class, always composed of the same families. . . .

In aristocratic ages the object of the arts is therefore to manufacture as well as possible, not with the greatest speed or at the lowest cost.

When, on the contrary, every profession is open to all, when a multitude of persons are constantly embracing and abandoning it, and when its several members are strangers, indifferent to and because of their numbers hardly seen by each other, the social tie is destroyed, and each workman, standing alone, endeavors simply to gain the most money at the least cost. The will of the customer is then his only limit.

2:50–51

40. Not that in democracies the arts are incapable, in case of need, of producing wonders. This may occasionally be so if customers appear who are ready to pay for time and trouble. In this rivalry of every kind of industry, in the midst of this immense competition and these countless experiments, some excellent workmen are formed who reach the utmost limits of their craft. But they rarely have an opportunity of showing what they can do; they are scrupulously sparing of their powers; they remain in a state of accomplished mediocrity, which judges itself, and, though well able to shoot beyond the mark before it, aims only at what it hits.

2:52

Limitations on quality of art in a democracy

41. [In democracies] the number of consumers increases, but opulent and fastidious consumers become more scarce. Something analogous to what I have already pointed out in the useful arts then takes place in the fine arts; the productions of artists are more numerous, but the merit of each production is diminished. No longer able to soar to what is great, they cultivate what is pretty and elegant, and appearance is more attended to than reality.

In aristocracies a few great pictures are produced; in democratic countries a vast number of insignificant ones.

2:53–54.

Tendency to cheap art (or *kitsch*) in a democracy

Americans still subservient to English culture models, so lack creativity

42.   The larger part of that small number of men in the United States who are engaged in the composition of literary works are English in substance and still more so in form. Thus they transport into the midst of democracy the ideas and literary fashions that are current among the aristocratic nation they have taken for their model. They paint with colors borrowed from foreign manners; and as they hardly ever represent the country they were born in as it really is, they are seldom popular there. . . .

The inhabitants of the United States have, then, at present, properly speaking, no literature. The only authors whom I acknowledge as American are the journalists. They indeed are not great writers, but they speak the language of their country and make themselves heard. . . .

I am convinced that they will ultimately have one; but its character will be different from that which marks the American literary productions of our time, and that character will be peculiarly its own.

2:59

Prediction on future character of American literature

43.   In democracies it is by no means the case that all who cultivate literature have received a literary education. . . .

Taken as a whole, literature in democratic ages can never present, as it does in the periods of aristocracy, an aspect of order, regularity, science, and art; its form, on the contrary, will ordinarily be slighted, sometimes despised. Style will frequently be fantastic, incorrect, overburdened, and loose, almost always vehement and bold. Authors will aim at rapidity of execution more than at perfection of detail. Small productions will be more common than bulky books; there will be more wit than erudition, more imagination than profundity; and literary performances will bear marks of an untutored and rude vigor of thought, frequently of great variety and singular fecundity. The object of authors will be to astonish rather than to please, and to stir the passions more than to charm the taste.

2:62

44.   Democracy not only infuses a taste for letters among the trading classes, but introduces a trading spirit into literature.

In aristocracies readers are fastidious and few in number; in democracies they are far more numerous and far less difficult to please. The consequence is that among aristocratic nations no one can hope to succeed without great exertion, and this exertion may earn great fame, but can never procure much money; while among democratic nations a writer may flatter himself that he will obtain at a cheap rate a moderate reputation and a large fortune. For this purpose he need not be admired; it is enough that he is liked.

Effect of commercialism on literature in America

The ever increasing crowd of readers and their continual craving for something new ensure the sale of books that nobody much esteems.

2:64

45.   American authors may truly be said to live rather in England than in their own country, since they constantly study the English writers and take them every day for their models. But it is not so with the bulk of the population, which is more immediately subjected to the peculiar causes acting upon the United States. It is not, then, to the written, but to the spoken language that attention must be paid if we would detect the changes which the idiom of an aristocratic people may undergo when it becomes the language of a democracy.

Effect of culture on written and spoken language

2:68

46.   Besides, democratic nations love change for its own sake, and this is seen in their language as much as in their politics. Even when they have no need to change words, they sometimes have the desire.

Effect of democracy upon language development

The genius of a democratic people is not only shown by the great number of words they bring into use, but also by the nature of the ideas these new words represent. Among such a people the majority lays down the law in language as well as in everything else. . . .

2:69

47.   Poetry is the search after, and the delineation of, the Ideal.

Meaning of poetry

2:75

Best subjects for a non-imitative American literature of the future

48   I am persuaded that in the end democracy diverts the imagination from all that is external to man and fixes it on man alone. Democratic nations may amuse themselves for a while with considering the productions of nature, but they are excited in reality only by a survey of themselves. Here, and here alone, the true sources of poetry among such nations are to be found; and it may be believed that the poets who neglect to draw their inspirations hence will lose all sway over the minds which they would enchant, and will be left in the end with none but unimpassioned spectators of their transports.

I have shown how the ideas of progress and of the indefinite perfectibility of the human race belong to democratic ages. Democratic nations care but little for what has been, but they are haunted by visions of what will be; in this direction their unbounded imagination grows and dilates beyond all measure. Here, then, is the widest range open to the genius of poets, which allows them to remove their performances to a sufficient distance from the eye. Democracy, which shuts the past against the poet, opens the future before him.

As all the citizens who compose a democratic community are nearly equal and alike, the poet cannot dwell upon any one of them; but the nation itself invites the exercise of his powers. The general similitude of individuals, which renders any one of them taken separately an improper subject of poetry, allows poets to include them all in the same imagery and to take a general survey of the people itself. Democratic nations have a clearer perception than any others of their own aspect; and an aspect so imposing is admirably fitted to the delineation of the ideal.

2:77–78

American pompous style in public speech

49.   I have frequently noticed that the Americans, who generally treat of business in clear, plain language, devoid of all ornament and so extremely simple as to be often coarse, are apt to become inflated as soon as they attempt a more poetical diction. They then vent their pomposity from one end of a harangue to the other; and to hear them lavish imagery on every occasion, one might fancy that they never spoke of anything with simplicity.

The English less frequently commit a similar fault. The cause of this may be pointed out without much difficulty. In democratic communities, each citizen is habitually engaged in the contemplation of a very puny object: namely, himself. If he ever raises his looks higher, he perceives only the immense form of society at large or the still more imposing aspect of mankind. His ideas are all either extremely minute and clear or extremely general and vague; what lies between is a void. When he has been drawn out of his own sphere, therefore, he always expects that some amazing object will be offered to his attention; and it is on these terms alone that he consents to tear himself for a moment from the petty, complicated cares that form the charm and the excitement of his life.

2:82

50. The literature of the stage, moreover, even among aristocratic nations, constitutes the most democratic part of their literature. No kind of literary gratification is so much within the reach of the multitude as that which is derived from theatrical representations. Neither preparation nor study is required to enjoy them; they lay hold on you in the midst of your prejudices and your ignorance.

Drama: the art best suited for mass consumption in democracies

2:84

51. The present ruling class does not read and does not even know the names of writers. Now that it no longer plays a part in politics, literature has fallen in the eyes of the masses.

Political effect on popularity of good literature

Correspondence with Gobineau, 293

52. That breed of men which provided the greatest names in America, is disappearing. With them the tradition of cultivated manners is going. The people become educated, knowledge spreads, and middling ability becomes common. Outstanding talents and great personalities are rare. Society is less brilliant and more prosperous. The various effects of the progress of civilisation and enlightenment, about which only Europe is in doubt, can be seen as clear as day in America. . . .

Equality threatens excellence in a democracy: a great problem for Americans

Why, as civilisation spreads, do outstanding men become fewer? Why, when knowledge is accessible to all, are great talents rare? Why, when there are no lower classes, are there no upper classes either? Why, when understanding of government reaches the masses, is there a shortage of great minds to take the lead in society? America clearly raises those questions. But who can answer them?

Journey to America, 17

Conclusion: Making Use of Tocqueville Today

It is strange how so many Americans today ignore the future or hold it in disrespect and contempt. After all, to live in the past is another name for bad mental health, and to live in the present is a mark of the frivolous butterfly or self-indulgent egotist with his famous strategy to "eat, drink and be merry, for tomorrow we die." To be farsighted, enterprising, and creative, on the other hand, is to have the respect and admiration (or envy) of others.

Tocqueville was intensely future-minded, as should be very obvious, for reasons which these final excerpts from his writings illustrate vividly:

Governments must apply themselves to restore to men **In 1840** that love of the future with which religion and the state of society no longer inspire them; and, without saying so, they must practically teach the community day by day that wealth, fame, and power are the rewards of labor, that great success stands at the utmost range of long desires, and that there is nothing lasting but what is obtained by toil.

When men have accustomed themselves to foresee from afar what is likely to befall them in the world and to feed upon hopes, they can hardly confine their minds within the precise limits of life, and they are ready to break the boundary and cast their looks beyond.

2:160

The last century had an exaggerated and somewhat **In 1853** childish trust in the control which men and peoples were supposed to have of their own destinies. It was the error of those times; a noble error, after all; it may have led to many follies, but it also produced great things, compared to which we shall seem quite small in the eyes of posterity. The weary aftermath of revolutions, the weakening of passions, the miscarriage of so many generous

ideas and of so many great hopes have now led us to
the opposite extreme. After having felt ourselves capable of transforming ourselves, we now feel incapable of
reforming ourselves; after having had excessive pride,
we have now fallen into excessive self-pity; we thought
we could do everything, and now we think we can do
nothing.

Correspondence with Gobineau, 231–32

Tocqueville is warning us here, tactfully, that the future belongs to
those who think about it and plan for it. A nation that ceases to plan
for the future, and to anticipate it eagerly, has grown old and its days
are numbered. However, social decay is not inevitable at any given
time; Rome endured a thousand years, while Genghis Khan's vast
empire fell apart at his death.

A nation dies when it ceases to be interested in its future growth.
And when a nation dies, the capacity of each ordinary citizen to care
for his own affairs is terribly reduced—and warped. Good parents
would not wish for their children to discover facts like this solely by
direct experience. The cost is too great, especially when we have a
usable past at hand from which to learn.

Moreover, it is nonsense to say that the future is unpredictable.
We may safely predict death and taxes, technological advances, war
and peace, gratitude and ingratitude with varying degrees of speci-
ficity. Those who do this well we consider leaders; those who don't
do it at all we think of as irresponsible witlings or failures. The future
is really no more mysterious or beyond comprehension than are the
past or the present, neither of which is perfectly known or understood.

Americans have long been accustomed to responding quickly
and capably to sudden changes—in fact they have enjoyed it. It is
probably true that they have been much less effective in detecting,
planning for, and controlling the gradual long-range changes. Yet
even here Americans have a respectable record. The three most active areas of traditional American long-range planning "assistance"
or controlling of future developments are the growth planning of
American business leaders, the social planning of American social
reformers, and the educational and retirement planning of most
American family heads. Even government policy sometimes shows
capacity for long-range planning, specifically in protective tariff policy, conservation of natural resources, and perhaps military defense.

Future-mindedness requires a love of humanity in all its age generations. The completely selfish person never has it; he asks, "What has posterity done for me?" dismissing what his parents did for him when *he* was posterity. The greatest nightmare of all intelligent fears for the future is that the future itself will be entirely ignored.

The exceptional usefulness of Tocqueville is a direct consequence of his future-consciousness. As we now are in a position to see, a remarkably high percentage of his prophecies have proved correct.[39] Tocqueville believed that only God was capable of seeing the immense mass of details which make up history in perspective; therefore, human beings must generalize. Only God could see the future clearly. Hence, mortals must predict and plan, however flawed their efforts might be. There is no space here for a detailed exposition of Tocqueville's ideas about the need for prediction, how to go about it, and the limits to its effectiveness.[40] But one should underline the importance of optimism for prediction. "It is not the pessimist who changes the world but the optimist," says G. K. Chesterton.[41] Optimists eagerly explore the future and base their plans for a better life upon it. Pessimists, frightened of the future, try to forget it altogether.

Many authorities have placed emphasis upon the value of Tocqueville's words for national leaders and makers of policy, with much justice. But the greatest benefits are to be gained by the average voting citizen and the community or small group leader. These were the Americans whom Tocqueville most admired, the people who made local government and voluntary associations function effectively as an intelligent check to the abuses of democratic power—but only if they understood what they were doing, and how important they really were. He most nearly approached despair at the specter of these people becoming a superficially educated group who hated to read or struggle with ideas and "think of nothing but interests."[42] Democracy rises or falls as its citizens put their best, or their least, into it.

Unfortunately, our modern civilization does very little to help the average capable person use a portion of his leisure for reflection and tentative predictions about our national and human future. Take the social service state—how far can we entrust our future to it without searching, regular inquiry and reflection on risks and alternatives? The English socialist Harold Laski said it was Tocqueville who first made him aware that at some point the economic development of every State is going to halt or slow down massively, and that such conditions might well make "taxation of the rich for the benefit of the poor . . . an impossible venture."[43] What then would become of the social service state and those who depended on it? Should we at some point start developing preliminary strategy for this unwel· come prospect?

Tocqueville did his thinking by making use of his own personal experience plus comparative reading, focusing upon social aspects of general problems, with concluding discussion and reflections which made him wise and useful. He studied not as a theorist, but "as a patriot" or actively interested citizen. Is this impossible today? Have "shared values" and "institutional engineering" skills suddenly vanished from America?

It is possible that modern Americans expect too much of the formal school system, elementary, secondary and higher. Very few capable Americans would feel easy about crediting the classroom with more than a small fraction of their usable knowledge and wisdom. Most of our education is still self-education through selective reading, direct experience on the job and in the marketplace, and discussion with intelligent friends and acquaintances. Probably selective reading is the weakest link in this chain, under modern conditions. No wiser selection could easily be made for useful reading than *Democracy in America.*

Tocqueville can be read in privacy, with maximum opportunity for personal reflection. Or he can be read in conjunction with a few interested friends or family members. Or he can be made the program centerpiece in a literary society or similar associational group. All these are familiar forms of self-education, more or less commonly available. Or seminars on Tocqueville can be arranged under college auspices or by quality-conscious high schools and preparatory schools.

The results could be surprising—an appreciation of the policy-making techniques of leadership in democracy, and a basis for sensible optimism about the future. Such understandings pave the way to a more active role in community revitalization by citizens. Doing something is an old and treasured American custom, ever so much better than doing nothing at all.

Notes

1. The only good biography in English is Jacob Peter Mayer, *Alexis de Tocqueville* (New York and London, 1940), published as *A Prophet of the Mass Age: A Study of Alexis de Tocqueville.* Since this work is hard to find, most will turn to a good encyclopedia for a capsule account.

2. Charles Eliot Norton, "Alexis de Tocqueville," *Atlantic Monthly* (November 1861): 551.

3. "Posthumous Writings of Alexis de Tocqueville," *Edinburgh Review* 122 (October 1865): 460.

4. Daniel Coit Gilman, "Alexis de Tocqueville and His Book on America —Sixty Years After," *Century Magazine* 56 (September 1898): 704.

5. Edward T. Gargan, "The Formation of Tocqueville's Historical Thought," *Review of Politics* 24 (January 1962): 48. The original quotation was a statement about the German historian Wilhelm Dilthey by his daughter.

6. "Alexis de Tocqueville," *North American Review* 95 (July 1862): 142; and Norton, "Alexis de Tocqueville," 552.

7. The greater part of the page in *North American Review,* cited in the previous footnote, reveals this as does any detailed discussion of Tocqueville's youth and adolescence.

8. Gilman, "Tocqueville and His Book," 707–09.

9. For example, "Alexis de Tocqueville"; Henry Reeve, "Remains of Alexis de Tocqueville," *Edinburgh Review* 113 (April 1861): 432–36. The detail on the father's hair turning snow white is from William Ebenstein, *Great Political Thinkers: Plato to the Present* (New York, 1964), 523.

10. See Ebenstein, *Great Political Thinkers,* 525; David Paul Crook, *American Democracy in English Politics* (Oxford, 1965), chap. 5, especially pp. 171–72, 187–88, 192; Robert Nisbet, "Many Tocquevilles," *American Scholar* 46 (Winter 1976): 61. The quoted phrase is Harold Laski's, in *Social and Political Ideas of Some Representative Thinkers of the Victorian Age,* ed. F.J.C. Hearnshaw (London, 1935), 101.

11. Reeve, "Remarks of Alexis de Tocqueville," 442.

12. Norton, "Alexis de Tocqueville," 155–56; Reeve, "Remains of de Tocqueville," 159–61.

13. Melvin Richter, "Tocqueville on Algeria," *Review of Politics* 25 (July 1963): 364.

14. Patrice Higonnet, "Alexis de Tocqueville, 1806–1859," *Abroad in America: Visitors to the New Nation, 1776–1914* (Reading, Mass.: 1976), 54.

15. Crook, *American Democracy in English Politics,* 166–68; Edward Everett, "De Tocqueville's *Democracy in America,*" *North American Review* 43 (July, 1836): 178–84; Nisbet, "Many Tocquevilles," 59.

16. For quoted phrases, see Tocqueville letters printed in "Posthumous Writings of Tocqueville," *Edinburgh Review* 122 (October 1865): 476. Seymour Drescher, "Tocqueville's Two Democracies," *Journal of the History of Ideas* 25 (April 1964): 201–204, discusses the importance of Tocqueville's increasing use of generalization, in his writings on America.

17. David Riesman, "Tocqueville as Ethnographer," *American Scholar* 30 (Spring 1971): 174–87. The composite quotation is derived from phrases on pp. 175–76 and 174.

18. Nisbet, "Many Tocquevilles," 61.

19. Crook, *American Democracy in English Politics,* 185.

20. *Ibid.,* 176.

21. "Poussin on American Democracy," *North American Review* 52 (April 1841): 529–33.

22. Crook, *American Democracy in English Politics,* chap. 5; Everett, "De Tocqueville's *Democracy,*" 178–82; Norton, "Alexis de Tocqueville," 551.

23. Henry Steele Commager, *The Search for a Usable Past* (New York, 1966), 195.

24. Modern comments upon his sociological role include Paul R. Eberts and Ronald A. Witton, "Recall from Anecdote: Alexis de Tocqueville and the Morphogenesis of America," *American Sociological Review* 25 (December 1970): 1081–1097; Robert Nisbet, "Alexis de Tocqueville," *International Encyclopedia of the Social Sciences* 16 (1968): 90–95; George W. Pierson, *Tocqueville and Beaumont in America* (New York, 1938), 769–70.

25. Crook, *American Democracy in English Politics,* 166–68; Gilman, "Tocqueville and His Book," 703; Nisbet, "Many Tocquevilles," 59; Reeve, "Remains of de Tocqueville," 442.

26. See *Blackwood's Edinburgh Magazine* 48 (October 1840): 463–68; ibid., 61 (May 1847): 525–26, for early anti-Volume 2 reactions; Herbert J. Muller, *In Pursuit of Relevance* (Bloomington, Ind.: 1971), 185, note, exemplifies the reversed modern attitude. Drescher, "Tocqueville's Two Democracies," discusses reasons for the shift of attitude.

27. Nisbet, "Many Tocquevilles," 59–60.

28. Woodrow Wilson, "Bryce's *American Commonwealth,*" *Political Science Quarterly* 4 (March 1889): 154.

29. Nisbet, "Alexis de Tocqueville," 90; Russell Kirk, *The Conservative Mind* (Chicago, 1953), 188; Ada Zemach, "Alexis de Tocqueville on England," *Review of Politics,* 13 (July 1951): 329–43.

30. Nisbet, "Many Tocquevilles," 63–67.

31. Cited in Edward T. Gargan, "The Formation of Tocqueville's Historical Thought," *Review of Politics* 24 (January 1962): 48.

32. Higonnet, "Alexis de Tocqueville, 1805–1859," 61.

33. Denis W. Brogan, *French Personalities and Problems* (New York, 1947), 220.

34. "Democracy in America," *American Monthly Magazine* 12 (1838): 377, quoted in *Democracy in America* 2:427, Appendix 2.

35. Nisbet, "Many Tocquevilles," 74.

36. Joshua Leavitt, "American Democracy," *New Englander* 14 (February 1856): 59.

37. *Ibid.*,

38. Muller, *In Pursuit of Relevance*, 182.

39. Nearly all critics have been struck by Tocqueville's gift for extrapolative prediction. See Muller, *In Pursuit of Relevance*, 193–97; Theodore Draper, "The Idea of the Cold War and It's Prophets," *Encounter* 52 (February 1979): 32–45, for pros and cons. Lord Bryce was moved to write a small book, largely on the subject, during an early visit to America, *The Predictions of Hamilton and Tocqueville* (Baltimore, 1887) in *The Johns Hopkins University Studies in Historical and Political Science*, vol. 5, no. 9.

40. Edward T. Gargan, "Tocqueville and the Problem of Historical Prognosis," *American Historical Review* 68 (January 1963): 332–45.

41. G.K. Chesterton quoted in *The Happy Republic: A Reader in Tocqueville's America*, ed. George Probst (New York, 1962), 564.

42. Tocqueville to M. Preslon, 12 January 1858, quoted in Reeve, "Posthumous Writings," *Edinburgh Review*, 477.

43. Laski, quoted in Hearnshaw, *Social and Political Ideas*, 112–13.

INDEX

The bracketed numbers refer to the quotation.

About

the Author

Dr. Frederick Kershner, Jr. retired in August 1982 as Distinguished Professor of American Social and Intellectual History at Teachers College, Columbia University, and now resides in Zionsville, Indiana. He is a graduate of Butler University and also of the University of Wisconsin, where he completed his M.A. and Ph.D. degrees. He served on the teaching staff at Ohio University and was Fulbright Visiting Professor at the University of Sydney before joining Teachers College as a professor in 1957. Currently he is concentrating his research in the areas of immigration, citizenship, and culture as they affect American nationality and revising an earlier study, "American Influences in Australian Historical Development, 1787–1947."